The Privacy Poachers

How The Government and Big Corporations Gather, Use and Sell Information About You

Tony Lesce

Loompanics Unlimited
Port Townsend, Washington

These other fine books by Tony Lesce are available from Loompanics Unlimited:

- **The Big House: How American Prisons Work**
- **Espionage: Down and Dirty**
- **Escape from Controlled Custody**

JC 596.2
.U5
L48
1992

THE PRIVACY POACHERS
© 1992 by Tony Lesce

0 26558661

Published by:
Loompanics Unlimited
P.O. Box 1197
Port Townsend, WA 98368
Loompanics Unlimited is a division of Loompanics Enterprises, Inc.

ISBN 1-55950-086-7
Library of Congress Catalog Card Number 92-081233

Contents

1

The Birth of Big Brother

George Orwell's novel, *1984*, dealt with a little man, an average citizen being morally and intellectually strangled by a monstrous government tyranny personified by the leader, "Big Brother." This government had a monopoly on power, unlike reality today, several years after the real-life year 1984 has come and gone. Today, we have a variety of police and regulatory agencies ruling our lives and collecting information about us. There are also private agencies and bureaus intruding into our privacy. Official police at local, state, and federal levels employ 600,000 people, with total budgets of about $30 billion. Private security agencies alone have an estimated 1.1 million people employed, according to an estimate on page 41 of the March, 1991 issue of the security industry magazine, *Security Management*. Another estimate, quoted in the November 15, 1991 issue of *Law Enforcement News*, states that private security employs 1.5 million persons, with an annual budget of $52 billion. Add to these the many credit bureaus, insurance company employees, medical record-keepers, and assorted state and private bureaucrats, and we have a number as formidable as it is impossible to pin down. Today, the individual stands alone against a hundred or a thousand Big Brothers, hacking away at his freedom. Worse, the annual growth rate of private security is about 8%, twice that of official law enforcement, according to an editorial by Bruce Cameron in the December, 1991, issue of *Law and Order* magazine.

The 20th Century has brought about new and unprecedented threats to individual freedom, especially in the United States. Here, many people think that they're much freer than they are in reality. If you deeply believe that you have certain inalienable rights as an American, you'll find some nasty surprises within these pages. You'll find that some rights, which are so taken for granted that they're not enumerated in the Constitution, are being infringed both in the name of corporate profit and government control.

America traditionally was "the land of the free," but from the start, government was developing a heavy hand to use on its citizens. Shortly after the Revolution, the "Whiskey Rebellion" broke out over the right of farmers and brewers to produce their distillate without intervention and taxation by the federal government. The government won, although hill people continue to brew and distill on a small scale up to the present day.

The 19th Century offered many more opportunities for people who cherished their freedom and who wanted to remain free, to migrate west and make new starts. While the frontier was still open, people wishing to escape the crowding and regimentation of the East could find freedom in the wide-open spaces. The frontier was relatively safe, and despite the lack of profuse crime statistics, it is plain to see that the danger from marauding Indians was far less than from present-day street gangs in Eastern cities such as New York. Even Dodge City and Tombstone were not as wild as the waterfront districts of Eastern cities, where hijack gangs and river pirates abounded.

More importantly, people were far from the heavy hand of government regulation.

During the 20th Century, while some Europeans were expressing concern over the Americanization of Europe, a more subtle and insidious process happened: the Europeanization of America. While Europeans were agonizing over the introduction of the "Coca-Cola culture" into their homelands, Americans found their lives increasingly controlled and regimented. As long ago as the Civil War, the government had introduced a European practice: conscription. Draft boards registered all males of military age during both World Wars, the Korean, and the Vietnamese Wars. Each male was required to carry his draft card at all times, and this card served as a means of identification.

War required information about the enemy, and during the Civil War the U.S. Secret Service began under its first chief, Alan Pinkerton. The Secret Service and its sister agency, the late-arriving Federal Bureau of Investigation, continued the peacetime surveillance of American residents to root out "subversion." Spying upon citizens became routine, although the small size of the agencies limited their ability. After World War II, both agencies enlarged to an unprecedented degree in peacetime, because of the cold war. Electronic data processing made it possible to keep tabs on millions of people quickly and efficiently, with small staffs.

In 1913, the income tax arrived, and at first few were worried because they didn't earn enough to be subject to the tax. This soon changed, and today the Treasury Department's Internal Revenue Service, more than any other government agency, is playing "Big Brother" to many Americans. A draft board can't do much without a draft, but the IRS goes on forever because practically every wage-earner pays income tax today.

The Treasury Department got further into the act during prohibition, when a special unit, the "Untouchables," took to the field against Al Capone and other bootleggers. The Treasury's

Alcohol, Tobacco, and Firearms Bureau imposes taxes and regulates manufacturing, importation, and sales in all three fields. While ATF agents have performed valuable services in targeting armed criminals, especially with their "Achilles" programs, most agents' efforts are spent in enforcing nit-picking observance of technicalities by legitimate gun dealers and firearms hobbyists. The truth is that enforcing procedural violations against law-abiding citizens is far less dangerous than raiding armed criminals.

A unit of the U.S. Department of Justice has also become very intrusive, in its guise of fighting drug use. Originally established as the Federal Bureau of Narcotics, its name and initials changed through the years, copying the style of the Soviet Secret Police. The "FBN" became the "BNDD," the Bureau of Narcotics and Dangerous Drugs, and then the "DEA," the Drug Enforcement Administration. With each name change, its power and influence increased. Skillful propaganda has convinced many people that illegal drugs are the greatest threat in American history, justifying extreme measures. Drug use has now taken the place of Communism as the bogeyman of the 1990s.

The greatest dangers, however, come from events outside of public view. All government agencies maintain computer files, and despite Congressional resistance, agencies began sharing their files during the 1970s. Although Congress has not allowed the integration of distinct files into national databases, it's been happening under the table. Privately-compiled and maintained computer dossiers, such as those put together by the direct-marketing and credit industries, contain even more information about you, and their use is, in practice, beyond the reach of law.

2

Who Wants to Know About You – and Why

Big Brotherism, the imposition of total control over one's fellow man, attracts certain kinds of people. What kinds? Obviously the ones who like to control others.

Such people are attracted to police work, as are those who like to avenge wrongs and others who seek adventure. Avengers and adventurers can find legitimate places in law enforcement, but controllers who drift into law enforcement often end up making life miserable for their fellow man.

Adventurers often join S.W.A.T. teams, where they get opportunities to go through doors and fight it out with the bad guys. Avengers who get into criminal investigation can unravel bizarre and puzzling crimes, to bring the perpetrators to justice. Controllers, by contrast, don't really care about the dangerous or exacting aspects of law enforcement. Going after armed desperadoes is dangerous, because they sometimes open fire against police officers. It's safer to target legitimate citizens, because they don't shoot back.

Big Brothers are always bureaucrats who have job tenure, not elected politicians. Politicians have better things to do, such as collecting campaign funds, paying back favors, and keeping high profiles so that they may be re-elected. The controllers are anonymous, and their job tenure doesn't depend on re-election every few years. Many work for private agencies and bureaus, anonymously, collecting information and controlling the lives of people they never see, and who may not even know the controllers exist.

Victimless Crimes

One way the Big Brother mentality shows itself is by creating victimless crimes, "offenses against morality," which serve as levers for control and prosecution. Many local "blue laws," such as Boston's ban on shining shoes on Sundays, have appeared, and are today either ignored because of their ridiculousness, or wiped off the books when legislatures revise penal codes. In New York State, for example, until the new penal code appeared in 1965, teenage masturbation was illegal. This was obviously not enforced, or the jails would have been full of adolescent onanists.

On the federal level, there have been serious encroachments on individual freedom through various federal blue laws. One of the first was the Comstock Act of 1873, originally aimed at pornography. In the form in which it passed into law, the sending of both obscene literature and contraceptive information through the mail became illegal. Only a century after it passed did the Supreme Court emasculate the Comstock Act, in the famous *Lady Chatterly* case.

The Mann Act of 1910 was aimed at interstate transportation of prostitutes, but a Supreme Court interpretation soon made it applicable to any unmarried couple eloping across state lines. The Harrison Act of 1914 made it illegal to use certain prescription drugs for non-medical (recreational) purposes, and led to the establishment of the Federal Bureau of Narcotics. The most troublesome of all, however, was the Volstead Act of 1919, a law enforcing the Eighteenth Amendment, the Constitutional amendment imposing prohibition. Banning consumption of alcoholic beverages, prohibition made possible the rise of big-name bootleggers and helped to shape the organized crime picture we have today. Although Congress repealed prohibition in 1933, the criminal empires did not go out of business. Having built up their power and economic infrastructures by catering to people's want for drink, they moved into supplying other illicit wants, such as gambling and narcotics. During World War II, the mobs were deeply into the black market, with the tacit support of millions of clients.

Today, drugs are in the news, because the federal government is in a position to control substances people put into their mouths or noses, or inject into their veins. A tremendous amount of public-relations hype has convinced many Americans that drugs are a serious threat, despite the absurdities in the government's policies. On one hand, drugs listed as "illegal" are banned, but legal drugs such as alcohol and tobacco are not only allowed, but taxed by the government. There is even a tobacco crop subsidy given to farmers by the Department of Agriculture. Private employers are even attacking employees' right to use legal drugs, such as tobacco, off-duty.

Guilt By Association

The Big Brothers in our society share the police mentality, which derives from common life experiences. Obviously, people of like interests tend to band together, and even form groups and associations to share their interests. Some, such as bird-watching clubs, don't attract the attention of the police. Others, such as fringe political parties, sex clubs, and various informal groups, are of definite interest to police officers at various levels. Federal police are interested in anyone who may be violating federal laws, or helping someone to subvert the United States.

The net result is that government surveillance includes not only those who have broken the law, but those who might because of their backgrounds, interests, associates, etc. One landmark policy statement was by U.S. Attorney General Robert Jackson, in 1940. He stated that it was necessary to maintain "...steady surveillance over individuals and groups within the United States who are so sympathetic with the system or designs of foreign dictators as to make them a likely source of federal law violation." This shows the sharp difference between what many people think of as the police function and the way law enforcement officials themselves see it.

To many, crime prevention is clearing away slums, poverty, and other degrading social influences that allegedly cause crime. This is a naive view, because many criminals do not come from slums, and many slum dwellers do not break laws. Other methods of crime prevention are increased physical security, such as burglar alarms, bars on windows, double-locked doors, etc. However, law enforcement officials have yet another view of crime prevention, surveillance of those likely to commit crimes, and entrapment of those who are predisposed to crime.

The result of this outlook is a frantic compiling of lists. There are lists of the relatives and friends of convicted criminals, lists of their neighbors, prison cellmates, and even lists of their victims and the witnesses who testified at their trials. There are lists of people who belong to various political parties and organizations, those who subscribe to subversive publications, and in at least one bizarre instance, a list of spectators at the trial of a Black militant.[1]

List compilation and cross-matching is a legitimate police investigative technique. The TV viewing public saw examples of this in a short-lived police procedural series of two decades ago. This was *Dan August*, starring Burt Reynolds and Norman Fell. It may have seemed strange that, at the beginning of every investigation Reynolds asked his side-kick, Norman Fell, to compile several lists. These might be of people living in that jurisdiction who owned a certain make of vehicle, or who had been burglarized during the past year. Alone, each list meant little, but taken together, these lists narrowed the field of suspects, or allowed finding witnesses to a crime.

Case Study: The U.S. Secret Service

Included in the duties of the Secret Service is the protection of the president, vice president, their families, president-elects, presidential candidates, and some other people from time to time. This has been a very frustrating task, especially when a president has been killed. The Secret Service has, over the years, made a continual and energetic study of the type of person who kills presidents, to be able to identify and stop potential assassins before they strike.

Identifying Potential Assassins

The very small number of persons who have killed or made deadly attacks on American presidents has made it difficult to identify typical characteristics. Until 1975, all were male. That year, Sara Jane Moore and "Squeaky" Fromme tried to shoot President Ford, providing empirical evidence that potential threats now had to include both sexes.

Some popular writers, perhaps guided by the muddled thinking of Secret Service agents, described Presidential attackers as "loners." What this word is supposed to mean is unclear, especially because attackers varied widely in background, education, and social situations. Lee Harvey Oswald, for example, was a married man. Most others were single. It has also been "politically correct" to describe presidential attackers as mentally disturbed, or somehow alienated, to discredit them and deny their acts legitimacy. This further muddies the waters, because it suggests that the attackers' ability to think and plan may be insufficient. Actually, all successful ones planned well enough, and even the close misses, such as Collazo and Torresola, were too close for comfort.

The one characteristic shared by all but one attacker is what we can call the "Insignificant Nobody" syndrome, at the risk of creating another trendy term. Only John Wilkes Booth was renowned, as an actor. All others were what show business people call "nobodies." The nobody, by definition, blends in with the crowd, making him or her very, very hard to identify.

Another characteristic, which isn't very helpful in identifying potential assassins, is youthfulness. Practically all assassins and would-be assassins have been younger than 40, and many were in their twenties.

The president gets a lot of mail, some of which is hate mail, and in 1940 the Secret Service established its Protective Research Section to scrutinize threatening mail and track down the writers. Logically, a safe assumption is that someone who threatens the president in writing merits further investigation.

Federal law prohibits uttering threats against the president, providing a convenient hinge for prosecution. However, experience has shown that it's not enough to pursue and arrest people who make threats. There are other patterns of behavior which the Secret Service considers significant. In the case of Oswald, there were several items which, although they did not fit Secret Service criteria at the time, were obviously significant with hindsight. Oswald had defected to the Soviet Union, had an attitude of hostility and arrogance towards the United States, was pro-Castro, had lied during interviews with FBI agents, had contacted Soviet officials during a trip to Mexico, and most importantly, worked in a place which gave him a good sniper's view of the motorcade route.[2]

Another behavior pattern, which became startlingly clear after Arthur Bremer shot and paralyzed Alabama Governor George

Wallace, is "stalking." The Secret Service, which was responsible for Wallace's protection during his presidential campaign, examined newsreels and videotapes of the public appearances of all of their protectees, scanning crowd shots, and found Bremer's face in many of them. He had followed President Nixon around the country, and finally settled for Wallace, presumably because access to him was easier.

After the Kennedy assassination, the Secret Service obtained extra funds and officers to enlarge its Protective Research Section. Secret Service management realized that the original criterion, threats against the president, was not enough.

The Secret Service is now interested in anyone who utters threats against public figures, is a member of a subversive group that may be a threat to the president and other protectees, and others who for various reason are potential threats. This includes people who do a lot of complaining about the government, people who write abusive letters to the president, and people who try to personally contact high public officials for redress of imaginary grievances. The Secret Service is also interested in habitual gate crashers, as they may show up uninvited at government functions.[3]

The FBI now furnishes to the Secret Service the names of people who are subversive, fascist, rightist, or in political fringe groups, and who are also irrational or unstable. Other criteria are making threats against government officials, making bombs, showing violent tendencies, and behavior showing a "propensity for violence and hatred against organized government."[4]

Gathering Information on Potential Assassins

The Secret Service now has a computerized file, into which it enters information collected by its agents within the Protective Research Section, as well as referrals from other law enforcement agencies such as the FBI and local police. Although the details of its liaison with other government agencies are classified, it's safe to assume that, once a name shows up as a threat, Secret Service agents contact other agencies to dig out whatever information they may have on file about this person. Federal agencies include the Internal Revenue Service, as well as all police agencies. When the need involves a threat against the president, it's hard to see how any agency, federal or not, could refuse cooperation.

Case Study: U.S. Army Intelligence

This is worth a quick look, partly because it offers a parallel to the information-gathering of the U.S. Secret Service. During the 1960s, when there were many race and Vietnam War riots, U.S. Army Intelligence agents began recruiting informers, infiltrating peace groups, and gathering information on individuals and groups connected with the racial-equality and anti-war movements. There were lists of suspect organizations, lists of potentially suspect organizations, lists of subversive individuals, and lists of possible subversive individuals. In one instance, there was even a mug book containing photographs and histories of persons under suspicion.

One problem with these information gathering efforts was that they were very indiscriminate. Organizations listed in Army files included the League of Women Voters. Senator Edmund Muskie was one of the individuals.[5]

Another problem was the poor quality of the information gathered, because of the ineptness of the investigators. Some of the notations in individual case files seem stupid:

"Paranoid trends, not qualified for military service."

"Reported to be psycho."

"Known to have many known associates."

This is the sort of material generated by government paper-pushers who know that a case file's volume is more important than its contents. Paper mills generate paperwork by the pound, not the page, in the expectation that nobody will read the files, anyway.

Blacklists

Blacklists are, theoretically, illegal, except when the government keeps them. The U.S. Attorney General's subversive organizations list is one kept ostensibly for national security applications, on the basis that membership in one of these organizations may indicate a security risk in certain sensitive jobs. There is sound reasoning in this, because it would be very dangerous to have a member of a subversive organization with his finger on a nuclear button. However, in practice the government overdoes it, using the list to bar these people from all government employment.

More significant, because they're out of government control and public view, are blacklists kept by private companies and organizations. While their original purposes may have been legitimate, at times there are severe abuses. An example is the list kept by the insurance industry of people who file claims. The purpose is to disclose those who file more than an average number of claims, alerting investigators to possible systematic frauds, but they also serve to identify high-risk clients, people who may simply be unlucky.

The Employer's Information Service, of Gretna, Louisiana, keeps track of employees who have had work-related injuries.[6] This can, of course, be helpful in tracking cases of repeated fraud. It can also be useful in tracking careless, accident-prone, or simply unlucky people. This type of database can easily serve as a blacklist.

Doctors refer to their own blacklist of people who have filed malpractice suits against other doctors in the past. This isn't new. Well over a decade ago, "Telident," in Southern California, operated a service for doctors listing the names of patients who had filed malpractice suits. An extra feature was that Telident would also provide the names of doctors who had testified on behalf of the plaintiffs.[7]

This type of information provides a basis for declining to accept such persons as patients. However, the medical establishment, which has clout in Washington, has made sure that a government database of doctors disciplined for malfeasance or malpractice isn't available to the public. Information in the National Practitioner Data Bank will be available only to hospitals and health-maintenance organizations.[8]

Landlords are interested in rejecting people who might be troublesome tenants. To meet this need, one former deputy district attorney in Los Angeles formed a company to provide landlords in the area with information on such people. Gleaning information from court records, this man built up a computer database of persons who had had any sort of legal action filed against them by landlords. Unfortunately, some garbage had crept into his records. One man, who had paid his brother's rent for him one month, was named in court papers relating to an eviction order against his brother. From then on, he was stigmatized whenever he tried to rent an apartment. A woman who found that her newly-rented apartment was roach-infested gave her landlord notice. He countered with an eviction order. Her name went into the computer, and years later, she found it very hard to rent an apartment.[9]

It's understandable that a company executive may have an interest in detecting "troublemakers" and declining to hire them. This can mean a chronically absent employee, or one convicted of stealing from his employer. As we'll see, certain personal and medical characteristics can also preclude hiring. However, the corporate description of a "troublemaker" often includes members of labor organizations. Corporations and business associations keep blacklists of union members and activists, although this is strictly illegal.

Organizations that generate and maintain blacklists operate under innocuous names that tell nothing about what they really do. There are "employer's councils" purporting to promote "stability" in labor-management relations. "Stability" is a code word pertaining to combating labor unions, which often demand higher wages, benefits, and improved working conditions. Other private surveillance organizations have names which are even less informative, such as "ABC Services, Inc.," "XYZ Associates," and "Consolidated Services, Inc."

Paternalistic employers have been tyrannical in their surveillance and control of employees' private lives. Ford Motor Company set an example during the early part of the 20th Century. Ford's employee snooping division was called the "sociological department," and employed 100 investigators to visit employees' homes and report on what they found. They monitored employees' drinking habits, sex lives, household cleanliness, and how they spent their leisure time.[10]

At the time, it was common for employment applications to contain probing questions relating to personal habits and attitudes. These included smoking, alcohol consumption, and swearing and vulgar language. Some asked if the applicant had ever been divorced, to which organizations or churches he belonged, and who his political leader might be.

Some companies, even today, go further than merely trying to avoid hiring dishonest or incompetent employees. With rising health insurance costs, some are trying to weed out those who might make more claims and raise premiums. One 1982 survey by the U.S. Office of Technology Assessment found that 18 American companies at the time were using genetic screening to test for high vulnerability to toxins. This was, for the most part, job-related, because it enabled identification of employees who would be high risks in certain industrial environments. One genetic test was for the HDL gene, which influences cholesterol level. This also enabled companies to identify people who are more susceptible to heart attacks from high cholesterol levels. Other genetic testing can identify predispositions to other conditions.[11]

More recently, a woman was denied a disability insurance policy because her father had Huntington's Chorea, which is hereditary. This is an example of a trend of genetic discrimination, which can result in invasion of privacy. This may even result in a "genetic underclass," people rejected by employers, colleges, and insurance companies because of their genes.[12]

One company, Psychological Resources of Atlanta, Georgia, includes evaluations of "possible health risks," according to its sales literature. Although the company's testing does not include any sort of physical examination, and is based only on computer-scored psychological tests, a sample "Health Maintenance Report" provides an evaluation of a candidate's resistance to coronary artery disease.

Some prominent companies, such as the Turner Cable News Network, decline to hire anyone who smokes, even off-duty. Part of the reason is that smokers tend to have more health insurance claims in the long run. The Ford Meter Box Company of Wabash, Indiana, fired Janice Bone and her son, both of whom worked for Ford. How did the company know that they smoked off-duty? Compulsory urine tests turned up evidence of tobacco use.[13]

If you are a closet smoker working for one of these companies, you will live in constant fear of discovery, depending on how closely your employer monitors his employees on and off the job. A company security guard walking among the cars in the employee parking lot may report a vehicle if he notices a pack of cigarettes laying on the seat, or if he sees that the ashtray is full. If your employer ever discovers that you secretly smoke, as can happen during a mandatory urine test, you not only will lose your job, but probably will wind up on a secret blacklist of "troublemakers."

Criminal Histories

Police agencies compile criminal histories for obvious reasons. The FBI's Identification Division began operations in 1927, collecting criminal histories from local and state police agencies, but one of its main areas of interest was universal fingerprinting. All of these records, including fingerprints and photographs, are either in a computer or being converted to digital data, and will be available to those to whom the FBI allows access.

Criminal histories are only one facet of law enforcement agency records. Many police agencies, as a routine practice, keep a file card on any citizen they encounter. These can include crime victims, witnesses, and anyone stopped for casual questioning.

Scottish police have come up with a new feature, keeping records of anyone who is HIV-positive and who has a criminal history. Although some civil rights advocates have claimed that this is discriminatory, the Scottish Police Federation has taken the position that such information is "vital" to officer safety.[14]

Employers want to know who they hire. Areas of interest are job skills, personality, and criminal histories, if any. The reasoning, based on common human experience, is that past behavior is a good guide to predicting future performance.

Standard practice in checking for criminal history is poring over court records, using the applicant's listed places of residence to localize the search.[15] Federal and state records are available to those with the right contacts. As we'll see, private data banks maintain records of convictions, as well.

A person's criminal history is fairly easy to verify, and most subject to abuse. Employers worry over hiring convicted criminals not only because they might steal from them, but because of possible lawsuits from clients victimized by these criminals. An area of liability becoming more prominent in lawsuits is negligent hiring. In recent years, for example, there have been instances of nurses, such as Genene Jones in Texas, who killed their patients while working in hospitals. Although there was suspicion, there were no arrests or prosecutions until the nurses had found other jobs, and killed more patients. Their current employers were liable for negligent hiring, even though the nurses did not actually have criminal records.

Health care is only one field. A court found a trucking company liable for negligently hiring and retaining an employee who raped a client.[16] Another decision, in the case of Blum vs. National Services,[17] ruled a moving company liable for negligent hiring in the case of an employee who killed a customer's neighbor. Two day laborers who stole stock from a jewelry store had been hired by Manpower, Inc., and the court found Manpower liable for failure to investigate their criminal backgrounds.[18]

A serious problem with criminal history records is that there's no universal standard. Some jurisdictions keep only conviction records, while others maintain lists of anyone arrested, regardless of the disposition of the case. Thus, someone wrongly arrested may still have a criminal history following him through life, despite an acquittal or dismissal of charges. This can lead to some injustices, because a criminal history is a de facto blacklist.

A major problem is lack of accuracy, because there may be no requirement to keep records up to date, or expunge expired ones. A quality study of FBI criminal records showed that only 25.7% were clear, complete, and unambiguous. The rest lacked disposition information, or recorded it inaccurately. A further study of FBI warrant records (persons wanted) showed that 11.2% of the warrants were obsolete, and no longer valid.[19]

The lack of accuracy degrades all police and private activities relying on criminal history information. There are implications for the future, as well. One obvious and emotionally-loaded issue is sale of firearms to convicted felons. The "Brady Bill" calls for a seven-day waiting period while police check the prospective buyer for a criminal history. The alternative NRA-sponsored proposal, the Staggers Bill, calls for an instant computer check by the dealer. Both depend on the accuracy of the database, and if the information is wrong, the Brady Bill merely makes retrieving bad information slower.

Monitoring Public Movements

Police agencies view keeping track of large-scale public movements as a definite aid to crime control, by controlling the population. In Europe, residents are required to report address changes to the police, for example, and the repressive regimes have systems of internal passports.

British police have "HOLMES," the Home Office Large Major Enquiry System, a computer which records and correlates thousands of routine police reports. This system allows relating apparently unconnected events and drawing inferences. This allows tracking serial killings, for example, and makes other types of crime information more readily accessible. British police plan to link the entire country's police forces in a similar, but enhanced, computer network.[20]

HOLMES was the result of the Yorkshire Ripper investigation, in which there were so many clues and persons involved that correlating them was beyond human capacity. The perpetrator himself, for example, had been detained and investigated by six police forces, none knowing the reasons for other agencies' investigations. The computerized system allows relating seemingly different pieces of information and highlighting similarities.[21] There are other programs which are designed to do the same thing, as we'll see later.

Some smaller countries, such as Thailand, South Africa, and Israel, maintain highly sophisticated computer databases and a system of identity cards to monitor their populations. South Africa, while apartheid was national policy, used a computer system with identity cards to enforce travel restrictions on Blacks. Israel keeps close tabs on Palestinians living in occupied territories with a computerized work-permit card system.[22]

Governments are not the only Big Brothers. As we'll see when we study technological advances, there exists today hardware that can tell your employer exactly where you are in his facility, and how long you've been there.

Notes

1. *No Place to Hide*, Alan LeMond and Ron Fry, New York, St. Martin's Press, 1975, p. xxiv.

2. *Report of the Warren Commission on the Assassination of President Kennedy*, New York, Bantam Books, 1964, p. 419.

3. *No Place To Hide*, p. xiv.

4. *Warren Report*, p. 438.

5. *No Place To Hide*, pp. 206-232.

6. *Time Magazine*, November 11, 1991, p. 34.

7. *Low Profile*, William Petrocelli, New York, McGraw-Hill, 1981, p. 49.

8. *Newsday*, January 2, 1990.

9. *The Rise of the Computer State*, David Burnham, New York, Random House, 1983, pp. 34-35.

10. *Privacy in America*, David F. Linowes, Chicago, IL, University of Illinois Press, 1989, p. 31.

11. *Ibid.*, p. 15.

12. *Philadelphia Inquirer*, November 17, 1991.

13. *Smokers' Advocate*, June 1991, p. 6.

14. *Law and Order*, November, 1991, pp. 6-7.

15. "Checking the Personals," William A. Sharp, *Security Management*, April, 1991, p. 42.

16. Lyon vs. Carey, 385 F. Supp. 272, 274 DDC 1974.

17. Circuit Court, Montgomery, MD, 1975.

18. Becker vs. Manpower, Inc., 532 F. 2d 56 57, 7th Circuit Court.

19. *Dossier Society*, Kenneth C. Laudon, New York, Columbia University Press, 1986, pp. 139-142.

20. *Privacy in America*, p. 4.

21. *Law and Order*, November, 1991, pp. 50-52.

22. *Time Magazine*, June 24, 1991, p. 62.

3

How Big Brother Collects Information

The main point to remember is that the big danger from Big Brother is not wiretapping or other forms of direct electronic surveillance. It's the systematic collection of information he already has about you, obtained from yourself![1]

Paperwork You Provide

During your life, you fill out many forms with personal information. Whenever you apply for employment, a passport, auto loan, mortgage, insurance, drivers license, credit card, etc., you provide the grantor a profile of yourself. It may be an educational and work history, or it may be your driving record. It may be your health history, or a report on your financial health.

When you apply for a credit card or a loan, you have to provide a fairly complete financial summary, as well as information on your work, lifestyle, family, property, etc. Credit companies have found that certain characteristics are linked with good payment records. Where you live, what you do for a living, and other characteristics have predictive value, because electronic computers today allow correlating repayment records with a large number of factors to find the ones which match best.

All of these remain in the files, somewhere, and even if eventually the paperwork goes through a shredder, the information will endure on a magnetic disc or tape. States regularly sell lists of motor vehicle owners to commercial exploiters, such as automobile magazines, who then try to solicit subscriptions from them. Magazines also sell their subscription lists. At some future date, this information may even be used against you.

Market Research

Market research organizations regularly mail out questionnaires, using inducements for cooperation. Some mail questionnaires in shotgun mailings, promising a chance at a big prize to those who return them properly filled out. Others promise temporary employment in a "market survey" program. Topics covered in these questionnaires include your family income, shopping habits, whether you rent or own your home, number of motor vehicles in family, children in school, your occupation, spouse's occupation, and big-ticket items you own or plan to buy soon.

One pregnant woman filled out a card she'd found in her doctor's waiting room, and soon received a vast amount of mail solicitations. At first, she thought that her doctor had breached confidence and sold her name to a market research agency.[2]

First Foto, in Red Bank, New Jersey, is a subsidiary of Hasco, Incorporated, a company which shoots about 1.6 million nursery photos per year in hospitals. When parents order these first snapshots of their newborns, their names and addresses go into a data bank, and this information passes to commercial marketers such as diaper and baby food manufacturers. Another company, Metromail Corporation, of Lombard, Illinois, gathers information from several sources. Its employees clip birth announcements from newspapers, collect names from childbirth instructors, and buy lists of names from companies that furnish baby supplies.[3]

Many "free" publications furnished to doctors and others are actually attractive bait to obtain names for specialized mailing lists. Anyone filling out a business reply card will end up on somebody's mailing list, and his name and address soon will be up for sale, along with many others.

Carol Wright, a direct-marketing organization in Lincoln, Nebraska, includes a "Shopper's Survey" with the Sunday newspaper. This promises an entry in a "sweepstakes" for 101 prizes, including a cruise to the Bahamas. To be eligible, entrants need only fill out their names and addresses, as a paragraph of fine type states. The survey form, though, lists many more items than name and address. Among the items this form covers are gender, smoking habits, type and brand preference of cigarettes, how often entrants eat diet foods, how often they eat at various fast food outlets, use of non-prescription remedies, use of prescription drugs, whether anyone in the household has dry or scaly scalp, type of shampoo used, contributions towards charities, amount spent on mail-order shopping, use of credit cards, including dollar amount, other buying habits, value of house owned, occupations of wage-earners, number and ages of children, and others living in the household. Other questions ask if anyone in the household speaks Spanish, has diarrhea, allergies, or stomach problems. A "Tell Washington What You Think" section on the front of the flier asks entrants' opinions on political candidates' campaign practices, campaign funding, candidates' health, and candidates' personal lives. In practice, this allows correlation of buying habits with political beliefs.

Survey Savings, of Hanover, Maryland, also produces questionnaires and induces consumers to fill them out completely with a promise of "valuable coupons, special offers, and samples." These questions cover health topics, and remedies used, including contraceptives. Also covered are contributions to political and religious organizations, as well as smoking habits and brands of beer consumed.

Many manufacturers now try to obtain information directly from people who buy their products. One favorite trick is to turn the warranty registration card into a questionnaire. Instead of asking only for the buyer's name and address, and the date he bought the product, the registration card or form now lists many questions of a personal nature. The registration form that comes with the new F117A Stealth Fighter computer simulation game, for example, asks questions about the customer's equipment, his age, and his family income. The information you provide when you fill out a warranty card ends up with National Demographics & Lifestyles, a market research compiler that sells this information to its subscribers.[4]

One Arizona supermarket chain, Smitty's, offered free food items to those who filled out applications for their "Shopper's Passport." The Shopper's Passport is a bar-coded plastic card that entitles the bearer to small discounts off a list of supermarket items. Clerks are trained to ask each person at the checkout for the Shopper's Passport each time. The laser scanner registers the barcode, and the store's computer builds up a list of what each person buys, and how often. This system allows pinning down sales of individual items to specific persons and dates.

"Privacy"

Some government departments and private organizations give lip service to concerns for "privacy," but there are enough exceptions to cause concern. One insurance company, the Ohio Casualty Group, includes a privacy statement with all of its policies. This blandly worded statement is very revealing, although it provides no details. It states that Ohio Casualty obtains information about you from your application, state motor vehicle records in the case of auto insurance, and employs outside investigators to obtain further information. They may interview your family, friends, neighbors, and "associates," a word which takes in everybody else you know.

The very interesting part is the list of parties to which the company will reveal its records on you. Those whom the company feels are entitled to see your records are your insurance agent, an appraiser or adjuster, an insurance industry bureau designed to combat fraud, insurance research organizations, courts, and other government agencies. This list is so extensive that the word "privacy" becomes meaningless. In effect, you have no privacy left. Information in their files can stigmatize you for years after it's gathered, and has become obsolete. Insurance companies also tend to turn down anyone who's been turned down by another insurer.

This is, unfortunately, common industry practice. Perhaps the only people who would be denied access to your records are juveniles, vagrants, and those confined in prisons or mental hospitals.

Employment Records

Employment applications can be simple for low-paying jobs, or quite comprehensive for higher-paying and sensitive jobs. Of course, no employer can make you disclose anything you don't want to, but he doesn't have to hire you, either.

If you apply for any employment that requires a security clearance, you'll have to fill out a very comprehensive form listing every job you've ever had, every address where you've ever lived, educational history, medical history, criminal history, whether you've ever had psychiatric treatment, etc. You'll also have to submit to fingerprinting. Government agents will check you out before you get a security clearance.

Some employers require applicants to take physical examinations before hiring. Others employ company doctors or psychologists to help employees with health problems. If you ever submit to a medical examination as a condition of employment, keep in mind that the usual doctor-patient confidentiality goes out the window. The company doctor reports to his boss — the company — and informs management of anything it's in their interest to know.

Likewise if the employer requires you to take psychological tests. Some testing companies provide a battery of tests designed not only to measure intelligence and ability for a particular task, but to assess your personality. Mass psychological testing, like the now-discredited polygraph, is one of the most prolific areas for charlatanism today. Most of these tests consist of up to 200 questions that are either true-false or multiple choice. It takes only a few wrong answers to earn the label of "psychopathic personality," or a similar diagnosis. Once the label sticks to you, it's very hard to get it off.

There's good reason for believing that these tests are worth little, if anything. The U.S. Congress Office of Technology Assessment released *The Use of Integrity Tests for Pre-employment Screening* on September 26, 1990. This study, at least two years in the making, cast grave doubts on the value of so-called "integrity" or "honesty" tests. Predictably, there was an immediate reaction from those who make a living from these tests. Several employees of the Association of Personnel Test Publishers wrote an attack on this study, appearing in the January, 1991, issue of *Security Management*. A letter replying to the article's criticisms appeared in the April issue, pointing out that a background check is far better than any pencil-and-paper test, and that these tests provide only "limited" contributions.

Employers are interested in more than simply keeping troublemakers or mentally ill people off their payrolls. There's a market for tests measuring specific personality traits, and some companies are setting out to meet this need. London House, a psychological testing firm, promises more than "honesty" testing. This firm advertises the Personnel Selection Inventory, which it states measures "a range of desirable work attitudes." London House also advertises customized tests.[5]

Large employers who can afford the outlay obtain customized personality tests designed for their particular operation. This practice began during the 1980s when it was first possible to optimize a test for a special client by using a computer to correlate answers with job performance. The first step is to administer the test to all employees and to determine which answers the most successful and competent employees provided. This gives a rough profile of the "ideal" employee. Another stage, which can take several years to complete, is to test all applicants for employment. This allows what's called a "longitudinal study," matching types of answers with both success and failure on the job. A simplified example might be answers to the statement, "I read a lot." Statistically, those who answered "true" might have a 70% success rate in that particular company, while 50% those who answered "no" were fired for cause within three months.

It doesn't matter why these employees succeeded or failed, nor need there be any obvious connection between job performance and answers. The important point is that, if there's a strong statistical connection, it becomes possible to predict performance, and to hire only those who provide answers similar to employees who have done well. The other side is that it's possible to correlate certain answers to employment instability, lack of aptitude, or even personality problems that eventually cause severe interpersonal friction.

The main problem with these tests is that they often don't perform quite as well as their marketers state. Salesmen for psychological testing companies claim that they're very economical, with a cost per applicant of as little as $25, which is cheaper than a background investigation and much less costly than hiring an unsuitable person. As we'll see, however, it's often possible to fool these tests, just as it's possible to fool a polygraph. An Arizona Highway Patrolman who was convicted of extorting sex from a woman in return for not writing her a ticket was hired after he passed both a psychological screening test and a polygraph.[6]

Some people feel that these tests are too invasive, and that the questions are irrelevant to actual employment conditions. Salesmen for testing companies brush these objections aside, finding this easy in today's workplace atmosphere of compulsory drug testing and other invasions of privacy. What's almost as easy to brush aside is that these tests often don't work the way they're supposed to work, but in a manner that's not easy to detect.

With any sort of testing, there are two areas of concern: false positives and false negatives. If there are many false positives with pre-employment tests, employers will hire a number of applicants who are unsuitable employees. To prevent this, the tests are pejorative, erring on the side of caution and slanted to give a high number of false negatives. These are less obvious, because there's no way for an employer to know how many of the applicants he's turned away would have worked out to be successful employees. This is the invisible loss rate, depriving employers of suitable personnel, and contributing to the unemployment rate.

Another hidden problem with psychological test scores is the way companies derive them. Today, the trend is computerized scoring. You fill out the form, and your prospective employer sends it in to the testing company for computer scoring. Ostensibly, because scoring is by machine, it's free from ethnic or sexist bias, a major selling point in today's litigious atmosphere of quota hiring.

The real danger, however, is that the larger, more successful psychological testing companies are building up psychological profile databases on millions of people. Although the print-out goes back to the employer, and there may even be a "pablum" version for your eyes, the information remains in the tester's computer. A future employer, or other investigator, may be able to obtain your history of testing when he subscribes to the service. Any errors of judgment may return to haunt you for the rest of your life.

If you once admitted to being depressed, or harboring suicidal thoughts, you won't be able to escape your answers. If you ever revealed a homosexual orientation, this too will stick to you like glue, and in today's AIDS-hysterical atmosphere, may prevent you from obtaining employment or insurance. Insurance companies are among the largest data collectors, and there's a definite advantage for a company dealing in life insurance to know who's suicidal. A health insurance provider has a definite interest in high-risk groups, such as people likely to expose themselves to AIDS.

Labor laws at local, state, and federal levels limit the direct intrusions employers may make into your private life. No employer may ask you your religion, for example. However, as one applicant found when she applied for a job, the interviewer asked her a question about a forbidden topic. When she replied that this was illegal, he pushed his telephone in her direction and asked if she wanted to call the police.

Employers amass a lot of information about you after hiring. The W-4 you fill out for tax reporting purposes states the number of dependents you have. Your health insurance policy lists all family members covered, and often your employer will know of any additions to your family. Your attendance records will reflect the times you were ill, as will any health insurance claims you submit. Health insurance claims are often processed by your fellow employees, and your health problems can become common knowledge. There are also credit union records, employee payroll savings plans, and other benefits that provide your employer with windows into your life.

A survey by the University of Illinois showed that 80% of the corporations surveyed will provide personal information about their employees to credit bureaus, banks, and other finance companies. Half use the information in employee's medical records for employment-related decisions. 58% have drug testing programs, and 89% use drug testing in pre-employment screening.[7] A 1990 survey by the American Management Association showed that two-thirds of companies now use drug testing.[8]

As federal officials have found out, the public has accepted the view that illegal drugs are dangerous, and at least passively supports police actions against drug traffickers. Drug testing in the workplace also appears acceptable to most people. One poll of Arizona residents showed that 76% of the 606 people asked thought it reasonable. Six percent had reservations, saying it should depend on the nature of the job. Only 18% thought it unreasonable.[9]

If you fail a company-mandated drug test, this will go into your employment record. With the proliferation of information exchange among companies, the odds are overwhelming that this will wind up in a permanent file somewhere, accessible to anyone subscribing to the service.

Public Records

Birth records are the first step in verifying someone's existence. Marriage, divorce, and death records are also public records, and most are available from the state office of vital statistics or records. A listing of state offices, procedures for requesting records, and fees involved, is available in Appendix "C" of *Applicant Investigation Techniques In Law Enforcement*, Pages 125-140. Birth records of U.S. citizens born abroad are available from the U.S. Department of State's Passport Services Office, Washington, DC 20524, for a nominal fee.

There are several large companies that collect court records, entering the information into their computers for sale to their subscribers. Although it's illegal to ask how many times you've been married, this information, plus information on your divorces, is in public records. An employer who considers anyone who has been married and divorced more than once unstable will obtain this information from private compilers.

Driving records are also available by contacting motor vehicle bureaus in various states and in Canada. One of the new twists in this is that new federal rules tied to highway funding require the suspension of drivers licenses of all convicted of drug offenses. This can stigmatize you if you've got a drug conviction on your record. A list of motor vehicle bureau addresses is available in Appendix "F" of *Applicant Investigation Techniques In Law Enforcement*, Pages 149-157.

Motor vehicle registrations, with addresses, are available to private parties in most states for a nominal fee by applying to the vehicle registration office in each state. A few states, such as Arizona and California, have restricted this information to law enforcement agencies. The reason is that a couple of killers traced their victims this way. Addresses of state agencies, and fees they charge, are in the *License Plate Code Book*, published by Interstate Directory Publishing Company, Inc., 420 Jericho Turnpike, Jericho, NY 11753.

Voter registration lists are also public records, publicly available. They list every voter's name and address, and are valuable for finding people who try to keep very low profiles. Politicians, for example, although in the public spotlight, try very hard to keep their home addresses deep secrets. Still, their names appear on voter registration lists.

The U.S. Census Bureau has been gathering information about Americans since shortly after the founding of the Republic. At first, the goal was simply to count the population, but during the 20th century, goals have proliferated and become more ambitious. Today, a small proportion of households receive very detailed questionnaires, with a penalty attached for non-cooperation. This personal information goes into a computer, and is theoretically available only for Census Bureau purposes. Don't bet on it, though.

The U.S. Department of Transportation's Highway Safety Program lists all persons who either had applications for drivers licenses denied, and those whose licenses were revoked. This information is available to all state motor vehicle bureaus, to prevent someone with a black mark against him obtaining a license in another state.

The Department of Health, Education, and Welfare maintains a data bank on the children of migrant workers. Ostensibly, this is to facilitate the transfer of school records as migrant families move, but the data bank also contains other information, about immunizations, for example.

The Social Security Administration has a record of every job you ever had in which your employer paid Social Security taxes. This is valuable information which the IRS uses to verify a taxpayer's record.

The Bureau of Alcohol, Tobacco, and Firearms sells lists of current firearms license holders on magnetic tape to anyone who has the price. A price list and order form is available from:

Chief, Disclosure Branch
Bureau of Alcohol, Tobacco, & Firearms
650 Massachusetts Avenue N.W.
Washington, DC 20226
Phone: (202) 566-7118

Schools also are repositories of information about a subject's early life. All schools will release information by court order, most to police without a court order, and most to casual inquiries if the request is limited to attendance or degree granted, as in the case of a pre-employment check. One valuable resource, available to all, is the school yearbook, which often contains one or more photographs of each student. Yearbooks also contain information regarding students who are members of school clubs and associations, which can be valuable if the organizations are religious or political in nature. As there are obstacles to asking questions about religious or political preferences, an investigator can find a yearbook a gold mine if a subject under investigation is listed as a member of Students for a Democratic Society and the Hillel Club.

Even what you read can be incriminating, in the mind of Big Brother. This is why the IRS tried to discover which books some persons checked out of public libraries. The assumption is that a person's reading pattern, especially if they read literature the IRS deems "subversive," provides a lead to possible tax evasion.[10]

One outlandish example took place in 1956, when New York City Police were searching for the identity of the "Mad Bomber," a deranged person who left pipe bombs in public places. The Mad Bomber used powder from shotgun shells, and a simple wick, to produce his bombs, a technique which is very unsophisticated. However, police detectives were poring over New York City Public Library records, gathering the names of people who had checked out books on explosives and demolitions. They didn't realize that a person who had read such advanced texts would have been able to produce much more sophisticated and destructive devices. When police finally apprehended George Metesky, the bomber, he turned out to be a resident of Waterbury, Connecticut.

Privately-Compiled Records

Privately-compiled records and directories are more numerous than any government listings. They cover much more ground, and categorize people in ways that would not even interest the most avid secret policeman. Many are based on public records, and their reason for existing is to save private investigators the time and labor of poring through paper records at individual state, local, and federal repositories.

Newspapers and Newspaper Files

There are several clipping services which regularly scan newspapers for various types of items and collect clippings for their customers. These services subscribe to newspapers and keep their services current. Some categories of information they pluck are birth and death announcements, arrests, court convictions, divorce notices, bankruptcy filings, and others.

Newspaper files often contain valuable information, especially when correlated with birth, marriage, and death information. Obituaries, for example, often list survivors. Birth announcements list parents. Marriage announcements may have photographs. Many newspapers now have closed their files to the public, but police and private investigators can usually gain access. A new twist is that computerized databases now offer newspaper files on-line to subscribers, making a visit to the physical files superfluous. We'll examine these in Chapter 10.

Directories

Telephone directories and city directories are good guides to locating people. The telephone company lists only subscribers who don't request unpublished or unlisted numbers. City directories, such as *Cole's* and *Polk's*, list by address, and obtain much of their information by personal survey. Their surveyors go door to door, asking the names of residents. There's no obligation to answer their questions, but most people do. The city directory allows pin-pointing a person on a particular street, even if he's unlisted, by eliminating those who are listed, and concentrating on the blanks.

A computerized telephone directory, *Fast Track*, is now on the market, put out by NYNEX, the New York Telephone company. This covers customers throughout New England, and allows obtaining telephone listings in seconds on a small computer. The system is compatible with IBM or clones, including PC, XT, AT, and PS/2, with a minimum of 640K memory.

Right now, this is available in both public library and law enforcement versions. Both allow finding a listing by entering partial information, such as the telephone number or address alone. The law enforcement version has indicators to show which numbers are pagers and mobile phones. It also shows which subscribers have chosen to have their listings unpublished, but does not show the unlisted numbers themselves. A future version will show both listed and unlisted numbers.

A commonly-accessed computerized directory is *Metronet*, available through the CompuServe Network. Using a telephone number as a starting point, this service delivers the name, address, spouse's name, and other information. This includes some unlisted phone numbers.[11]

Privately-compiled Specialty Directories

Various privately-compiled directories provide sketchy biographical information on those who are listed. Perhaps the best known is *Who's Who*, but there are others, mostly compiled by business services and associations. *The Directory of Medical Specialties* lists every medical specialist in the United States. The American Medical Association publishes an annual register of members.

Public libraries contain business directories listing companies, their executive officers, concise descriptions of their product lines, and a summary of their finances. *The Thomas Register of American Manufacturers* is a 12-volume set listing manufacturers by product types. *Ward's Business Directory* lists about 90 thousand companies, including names, addresses, telephone numbers, number of employees, name of chief executive, and other information about businesses. *Moody's Manuals* provide even more comprehensive, in-depth information, including financial statements and stock information. All of these, and more, are in the reference sections of most public and college libraries.

The R.L. Polk Company produces specialized directories, such as the *Female Heads of Households.* Consumers Marketing Research, of South Hackensack, New Jersey, provides lists sorted by ethnic and religious criteria, such as Italian voters. One list consisted of German names, with Jewish-sounding ones deleted, for a seller of lederhosen.

Even your videotape watching habits are now subjects of scrutiny. Many videotape outlets compile records on the movies you rent. However, a 1988 law known as the "Bork Bill" prohibits disclosure without a court order. In practice, prosecutions under this law are extremely rare. It might seem innocuous to have people know that you rent Walt Disney films, but if you rent an X-rated tape, you might not want that fact available to anyone who pays a fee.

Credit card companies contribute to the databanks. American Express, for example, supplies full reports to credit bureaus. If you have an American Express card, you can be sure that your full record will be available to major credit bureaus.[12]

Information obtained on the incomes and buying habits of consumers enables generating mailing lists for companies providing products and services. The information is so comprehensive, though, that it's inevitably valuable to investigators. The

IRS tried to obtain marketing lists compiled by Donnelly Marketing Service, R.L. Polk, and Metromail, to compare the names of high-income earners with tax returns.[13] At the time, these companies refused to sell their information to the IRS, but there are other market research companies who probably did sell their lists, quietly, without fanfare.

A major problem is that these lists are widely available, and once out of the hands of the original compiler, can be reproduced indefinitely. Investigative agencies, both public and private, are accustomed to running undercover operations, working behind "fronts," to promote investigations. It doesn't take much imagination to understand that an investigative agency could easily set up a dummy company to obtain market information. Alternately, a corporation in trouble with the IRS could be persuaded to cooperate in return for leniency. Using a legitimate company as a front for obtaining marketing lists and other databases is a perfectly workable plan.

Medical Records

In principle what passes between you and your doctor is privileged information, just like the transactions protected by attorney-client privilege. This is particularly important to you today, because doctors keep much more complete records on patients than ever before. This is because of "defensive medicine" — their response to fear of lawsuits. Therefore, whatever information your doctor obtains about you should be especially secure from prying eyes. In practice, it's just not so.

First, medical information about you goes not only into your doctor's files, but to other parties, as well. If you're covered by medical insurance, the insurance company probably requested your medical history from your doctor, and for this you signed a release. Of course, you weren't forced to sign, but they weren't forced to issue you a policy, either. Your entire medical record, therefore, is also in the files of the insurance company, and from there it goes to a central office, such as the Medical Information Bureau. This is one of a great number of private databanks.

The stated purpose of the Medical Information Bureau is to combat fraud and misrepresentation. It does this by promoting an exchange of information among its members, about 800 insurance companies. When you apply for insurance, the company will check you out with the MIB. Likewise, whatever medical information you provide when you apply will go into the files of the MIB under the reciprocal agreement. Members are required to furnish any information they obtain, regardless of the sources, and the MIB does not itself investigate or verify the information. With 12 million medical histories in its computers, the odds are that yours is among them, if you've ever applied for life or health insurance.[14]

The MIB updates its records. So does your medical insurance company. Every claim you make on your medical insurance policy requires paperwork, a claim form from you, and a statement from your doctor. This lists the condition for which you sought treatment, the treatment given, the outcome, and, of course, the fee. All of this winds up in the MIB's computer. Although MIB policy is to release information only to member companies, this doesn't protect you very much. Every member company has its own policies on control and release of information, and some will allow private investigators free access. Mutual back-scratching works.

If you change doctors, your medical records don't automatically go with you. The doctor will keep them, and make a copy for you, either handing it to you or mailing it to your new doctor.

If, instead of having a private physician, you're enrolled in an HMO, or "Health Maintenance Organization," with a team of doctors taking care of you, your records are really the property of the HMO, not any particular physician. More importantly, your primary care physician is not working for you; he's working for the HMO, and he follows the policies of the party that signs his paycheck.

If you submit to a physical examination as a condition of obtaining life insurance, the doctor-patient relationship no longer applies. The doctor who examines you is working for the insurance company, and anything he finds out, or you tell him about yourself, becomes their property, not yours. Likewise if your employer has a company doctor or psychologist. Some employers even have "Employee Assistance Programs," to aid employees in distress, such as those going through divorce, depression, and other stressful problems. Anything you reveal to the "counselors" goes into your personnel file, which is often available to other employers.

If you enter a hospital for any reason, there are hospital records to fill out, and these can be very comprehensive. First, some hospitals don't rely upon your doctor's knowledge of your case, but take their own medical history, as well. Upon admission, you may be handed a form asking whether you ever had any of thirty or fifty diseases. You'll also be asked to list all operations, and all medical treatment you've ever had. Any entries your doctor makes upon your hospital chart remain the property of the hospital. He doesn't take them with him when he discharges you. Of course, he may make copies for his own files, but the originals remain at the hospital. Next, entries in your hospital chart come from many people, including laboratory technicians, operating room personnel, and of course, ward nurses. Some entries can be as casual as they are misleading. If you're "down" after serious surgery, the nurse may make an entry that you're "depressed."

Even outside of normal channels, your medical records may be available to police officers. One California prosecutor obtained a search warrant for the files of a Palo Alto psychiatric clinic, to search for the records of a crime victim.[15]

Another danger of outside scrutiny of medical records is that some "records" are casual jottings and notes for further inquiry, such as "suicidal," or "May have financial problems." To the eye of an investigator, these are leads, and even evidence, any of which he may choose to use against you.

A special danger comes with psychiatric records. A psychiatric history is still a terrible stigma in the last decade of the enlightened 20th Century. But if you go to a psychiatrist, this may be just as vulnerable to disclosure as anything else. If you're covered by medical insurance, and decide to make a claim, you've just compromised your privacy. From this point on, it's part of the record that you went to a psychiatrist. That's merely the good news. Many psychiatrists and therapists ask their patients to take a battery of tests which are at least as probing and intrusive as the most rigorous pre-employment questionnaires. There will be questions regarding your childhood, parents' arguments, your sex life, including any sexual deviations you might have. There will also be questions about your wife, and her sex life. There will be questions about your moods, insecurities, and inner thoughts, such as periods of unhappiness, suicidal thoughts, attempts, etc.

Unfortunately psychiatrists and therapists, as well as the tests they use, tend to be pejorative, seeking what's wrong with you, not what's right. Your psychiatrist's records are more likely to reflect your failings and anxieties than your successes and honors. It's certain that your record will contain entries relating, if applicable, to your bed-wetting, early fears, sibling aggression, anxiety dreams, family problems, and sexual irregularities.[16]

A psychiatrist may not respect the doctor-patient relationship. Psychiatrists and psychologists, as a group, tend to be very arrogant, filled with a sense that they know better than anyone else, and certainly better than their patients. They're also very skilled at rationalizing their own behavior, even when it violates medical ethics. One U.S. Secret Service agent had been having nightmares about being confronted by a faceless assassin, and he related their content to a psychiatrist. The psychiatrist concluded that these nightmares meant that the agent was himself the faceless assassin, and he called the Secret Service and gave them his diagnosis. This led to the agent's being excluded from the White House Detail.[17]

Other Sources

Gathering information, known as "raw intelligence," can take a lot of skill, but unfortunately, there's often a premium on speed and volume instead of accuracy. This is especially true of private efforts, such as the information collected by credit reporting agencies.

Private investigators of various types have poor reputations that not all of them deserve. Many do use shady or sleazy tactics, mostly based on deception, to obtain information. Some will actually steal information, or obtain it by electronic bugging.

Some private parties don't hesitate to use shady and even illegal means to scrutinize confidential records. One grand jury investigation in Denver, Colorado, revealed that a private investigative agency obtained medical records by having its agents pose as doctors and nurses to gain access. Others bribed hospital employees for confidential information.[18]

Informants

One very common technique is to interview informants, persons in a position to provide information about the subject. An "informant" is different from an "informer," a person who enters a criminal conspiracy to report back to the police, for pay or other considerations. The informant can be a friend, neighbor, teacher, employer, fellow employee, tradesman, etc., who knows you and who can provide information about you and your lifestyle.

A common technique is the "background investigation." When you apply for employment with the government or with a major company, you can be sure that investigators will be tracking down your past, with a diligence that varies with the agency or the individual investigator. The beginning is a worksheet, based upon a form you fill out, listing every school you attended, every place you lived, and every job you held. The government demands a complete history. Private companies often ask for only the last ten or twenty years. An investigator will contact some or all of the persons and companies listed on the form. If the job you're seeking involves a security clearance, an investigator will check you thoroughly, to be sure that you actually were born where you say you were. He may even compare hospital records, to see if your listed blood type checks with your blood type today. He'll interview former teachers, look at your photo in school yearbooks, and check out other sources to be sure that you are who you say, and have done what you stated.

Not all investigations are as thorough as we'd expect. In one case, the author was listed as a reference by a friend who had applied for employment with the Drug Enforcement Administration. An FBI agent contacted the author by telephone to obtain a report on the applicant's moral character and general suitability for employment. This can produce misleading results if the person listed as a reference is an imposter.

Sometimes, simple human error can produce a false report. One investigator checking out an individual seeking a sensitive U.S. Army post interviewed a woman who reported that this person had been recently released from jail. Luckily, the man had been in the Army longer than that, and the investigator was quickly able to establish that the woman had confused him with someone else with a similar name.[19]

If an investigator digging out information about you interviews a neighbor with whom you've had a quarrel, or who is simply a malicious gossip, you can get a bad report without a chance of defending yourself. A malicious ex-girlfriend or ex-wife can paint a very unflattering picture of you. A jealous neighbor or relative can also bad-mouth you, in the hopes of derailing a job opportunity for you.

The alert and conscientious investigator knows of these problems, and checks damaging statements out with others before reporting them as facts. Confirming derogatory information is a basic investigatory technique, but private investigators don't always do this because they have to operate at a profit.

Investigators working for DISCO, the Defense Industrial Security Clearance Office, submit reports to an evaluator. The evaluator reads and ties together the reports of several investigators who may have worked on a single security check, which is why this second stage provides an objective overview of the investigation, and serves as a stopping point for catching errors and inconsistencies. The private investigator, however, usually does not have these checks. His report may go to a typist, and then to the client, without review by a superior or manager. This is another cost-cutting measure which risks passing invalid information to the client.

Milking informants is a standard technique. Both government and private investigators use it for different types of investigations. Even when it's not true, the agent will tell the informant that the subject has made an application for employment. This sleazy tactic often persuades a reluctant informant to disclose information.

Apart from this initial dishonesty in persuading informants to cooperate, private investigators sometimes slant their reports to convince the client that they're doing their jobs. As one person in the business put it, "We're in business to find bad risks."[20] Independent investigators who produce only favorable reports risk becoming unemployed, because if all applicants have good backgrounds, there may be no need to investigate them.

The Big Brother mentality surfaced prominently in Kansas City, where federal prosecutors have tried to compel relatives and friends of suspected mobsters to testify against them. U.S. Attorney Jean Paul Bradshaw II stated that this case was different because of recalcitrant witnesses. There were 20 men, all relatives and friends of those under investigation, who were offered immunity in return for their grand jury testimony. Although none of these was charged with a crime, they spent up to 18 months behind bars for refusing to testify against their relatives. Salvatore Mirabile, a spokesman for an Italian-American group, stated that the federal government's tactic is to imprison the relatives of people against whom they can't gather enough direct evidence to charge them for trial.[21]

Informers

Criminal informers are especially unreliable sources, but police and other investigators use them just the same. Informers who snitch for pay have a financial incentive to produce results, and some are driven by the urgency of a drug habit. The informer facing a criminal charge knows he has to give up someone else to save his own skin, and his truthfulness also may be unreliable.[22]

One example is the informer used by the FBI in the "Harrisburg Seven" trial, who testified that Reverend Philip Berrigan and his associates had conspired to kidnap presidential advisor Henry Kissinger, commit physical sabotage in Washington, D.C., and vandalize a number of draft board offices. Boyd Douglas, the informer, had a record as a bad check artist, and had sidled up to Berrigan in jail to elicit his confidences. The jury deadlocked, and the judge dismissed the charges.[23]

Some informers are more than mere snitches. Because their well-being depends on obtaining results, they sometimes act as "provocation agents," enticing their associates to commit crimes.

The Camden Seventeen was another case in which the FBI had done badly with its snitch. Robert Hardy, the FBI informer, persuaded the participants to burglarize a draft board office in Camden, New Jersey, after the FBI had furnished him with burglar's tools for the job. The judge instructed the jury that they could acquit because of this.[24]

Informers overstep their bounds in other ways, as well. Attorney-client communications are privileged, but when an informer is part of a group going through arrest and trial, he can take part in discussions with the defense attorneys. In one case, this led to the dismissal of charges against 15 people who had demonstrated at the Seabrook, New Hampshire, nuclear power plant.[25]

Undercover Agents

Police agencies use undercover agents for special investigations, such as infiltrating a group and reporting upon their activities. Investigations may be mainly criminal, or aimed at political groups, as well.

Private investigative agencies use a variety of undercover agents to service their customers. If you're a retail check-out clerk, an agent posing as a customer has surely already checked you out, reporting back on your courtesy, accuracy in making change, and honesty. Some undercover investigations have more serious ends. The General Motors Corporation hired 100 undercover agents from a private detective firm as assembly line employees. Their task was to report on alcohol and drug use among employees. The result was almost 200 arrests, mostly among GM line workers. The union complained that the investigative effort had concentrated on line employees, not management.[26]

Corporations employ private undercover agents to investigate employee theft, labor union activity, and drug use. These agents are hired in the same manner as other employees, and their task is to observe areas of interest to their client. If management is interested in employees who smoke, even off-duty, the agent's assignment will be to associate with as many employees as possible to find out what they do when they relax. If there's a nearby bar where employees gather after work, the agent will show up to observe who lights up. The agent may also find pretexts for visiting other employees, simply to see if they keep ashtrays at home.

The rationale behind undercover agents and "stings" is that the persons they catch are only those who are predisposed to crime, anyway. This isn't necessarily true. Both governments and private interests employ undercover agents for a particularly vicious type of entrapment known as "integrity testing." The agent proposes an illegal or unethical act to the subject. If the subject accepts, the agent denounces him. If the subject declines, he may still be in trouble if he does not report the attempt to his superiors. A New York City police officer found this out when he rejected a "deal" offered him by an undercover Internal Affairs agent. He was suspended for not reporting the attempt. Another New York City official went through a similar experience, for not reporting a bribe offer.[27]

Physical Surveillance

An extremely expensive, although fairly effective, way to find out where you go, what you do, and who you meet is to put a "tail" on you. The cheapest and simplest way for police to put a tail on you is if you're under strong suspicion of a crime, and the police don't want you leaving town. In such a case, the police don't care if you know you're under surveillance, and two or three officers will stick to you like glue. This is called the "close tail," in which keeping contact is more important than avoiding detection by the subject.

The "loose tail" keeps the subject under watch, but without his knowing he's under surveillance, even at the risk of losing him. This is for situations in which detection of a tail would compromise the entire investigation. Counter-espionage investigations are good examples of when loose tails are desirable. A spy or agent may spend several days simply walking around, doing nothing suspicious or incriminating, but at one moment, he might slip a roll of microfilm into his contact's hand as he walks by.

It takes a large team of agents to keep a subject under loose surveillance. For a good loose walking tail, at least five agents are necessary, complete with radios and vehicular back-up in case the subject takes public transport or drives away in his own vehicle. A team able to keep a subject under surveillance in all circumstances without being spotted, 24 hours a day, requires at least 30 agents. This is very expensive, and few investigative agencies have the personnel for such a lavish effort.

Physical surveillance is impossible for most investigations because of insufficient resources. It's not cost-effective for many of the rest. This is why it's so rarely employed in real life, unlike in fiction.

One type of physical surveillance is haphazard, but fairly effective because it's so common: field interrogation. Police officers have the right to detain and question anyone they observe under suspicious circumstances. If you're out for a walk late at night, a police officer may stop and question you briefly. He can, at his discretion, fill out a "Field Interrogation Card," listing your name, address, description, and other information. At the end of his shift, he turns this in, and your card, along with others, goes to the Criminal Investigation Department. Detectives working cases regularly scrutinize "F.I." cards, to see if anyone was near a crime scene at about the time the crime took place.

Before computers, F.I. cards remained on file for a limited time, depending on physical space available. Today, they can remain in a computerized file long after physical destruction of the cards.

Computer Surveillance

Some corporations are able to monitor employee performance by computer. The various telephone companies using ESS, Electronic Switching Systems, are able to tell how long each operator spends with each caller. Employees who do not process enough calls risk their jobs.[28] Any employee whose job involves a computer terminal is open to monitoring. Company management can record the number of operations or key-strokes per minute, and other standards of performance.

Companies using access control systems with magnetized cards can monitor where each employee is on the premises at all times. Magnetic card readers control access to every department, and admit only those authorized to be in each one. A central computer keeps track of each entry and each exit. One purpose is to prevent "pass-back," with one employee handing his card back to another to let him in. This practice sometimes leads to abuse of parking lot privileges. The central computer is programmed not to allow entry on the same card until after it records an exit.

Lures, Decoys, and Stings

Many people think of decoys as disguised police officers frequenting high-crime areas to arrest muggers who victimize them. This type of decoy operation is very dangerous for the decoy, who may suffer serious injury before his back-up officers reach him and apprehend the attacker. To the Big Brother type, this type of decoy is a no-win situation. Instead, Big Brother prefers a lure.

Fake prostitutes patrolling the streets, and police "sting" operations, are lures. The theory is that persons attracted to crime will approach, proposition them, and thereby make themselves vulnerable to arrest and prosecution. Courts usually support such measures, because they're simple and straightforward, very much like leaving the keys in a car to catch a would-be car thief. Police call these "pro-active" measures.

One example of pro-active enforcement was "Operation Looking Glass," conducted by the Postal Inspection Service during the middle 1980s, and targeting people who bought kiddie porn through the mail. The case began in 1977, when Los Angeles County Sheriff's Deputies found a 2,000-name customer list in a pornographer's home which they raided. This provided a "suspect list" for officers across the country. A raid on another porno producer yielded a shorter list in June, 1987.

Working from these lists, postal inspectors used direct mail solicitations advertising kiddie porn, as well as requests for pornographic accounts of child molestations by readers. They set up offshore mail drops and dummy companies as fronts for these "stings." Those who ordered kiddie porn faced arrest once they took possession. One individual, living in Phoenix, Arizona, responded by ordering material, but also by sending what amounted to a written confession of his molestation of a minor. His arrest and prosecution followed soon after.[29]

Police "Red Squads"

Local police agencies have had "red squads," units devoted to countering anarchists, subversives, communists, and other fringe political movements, for many decades. Often, police have been used against labor unions, breaking up strikes and picket lines. During the 1960s and 1970s, ghetto riots and

Vietnam War protesters stimulated the growth of red squads, even in police agencies which previously had none. A mass of files on political offenders grew, to serve as documentation for these special units.

One of the best-known police red squads is "BOSS," the New York City Police Department's Bureau of Special Services. This was originally the "Bureau of Special Services and Investigations," but the name was shortened during the 1960s. BOSS members have infiltrated fascist and communist organizations, peace movements, labor unions, socialists, and other political groups.

Police officers manning these red squads are as devoted to their work as other officers. Their value systems are the same conservative, blue-collar values shared by police officers everywhere. To them, their work is useful, countering what they see as threats to the American way of life.

The Real Threat

As we can see, although police and other investigative agencies use a variety of techniques, they use intensive surveillance on very few people. The real problem is not the violation of civil rights by over-eager police agents, but the over-collection and dissemination of information about you. Many agencies, public and private, obtain information about you unrelated to their functions.

Notes

1. *No Place to Hide,* Alan LeMond and Ron Fry, New York, St. Martin's Press, 1975, pp. 75-76.
2. *Privacy in America*, David F. Linowes, Chicago, IL, University of Illinois Press, 1989, p. 140.

3. *Wall Street Journal*, March 14, 1991. Article by Michael W. Miller.

4. *Time Magazine*, November 11, 1991, p. 37.

5. *Security Management*, June 1991, p. 10.

6. Statement by Sergeant Allen Schmidt, Public Information Officer, Arizona Department of Public Safety.

7. *Privacy in America*, pp. 41-43.

8. *Arizona Republic*, August 7, 1991.

9. *Ibid.*

10. *No Place to Hide*, p. 75.

11. *Wall Street Journal*, March 14, 1991. Article by Michael W. Miller.

12. *Consumer Reports*, November, 1991, p. 719.

13. *Privacy in America*, p. 90.

14. *Ibid.*, pp. 116-117.

15. *Low Profile*, William Petrocelli, New York, McGraw-Hill, 1981, p. 72.

16. *Ibid.*, p. 74.

17. *Confessions of an Ex-Secret Service Agent*, George Rush, New York, Pocket Star Books, 1991, p. 203.

18. *Privacy in America*, p. 116.

19. *No Place to Hide*, p. 110.

20. *Ibid.*, p. 112.

21. Associated Press, October 24, 1991.

22. *Deep Cover: Police Intelligence Operations*, Burt Rapp, Boulder, CO, Paladin Press, 1989, pp. 33-39.

23. *No Place to Hide*, p. 115.

24. *Ibid.*

25. *Under Cover: Police Surveillance in America*, Gary T. Marx, Berkeley, CA, University of California Press, 1988, p. 149.
26. *Privacy in America*, p. 15.
27. *Under Cover*, p. 139.
28. *Privacy in America*, p. 7.
29. *How To Use Mail Drops For Privacy and Profit*, Jack Luger, Port Townsend, WA, Loompanics Unlimited, 1988, pp. 45-47.

4

Does the Law Protect You?

There have been many laws protecting individual liberty in the United States, starting with the Bill of Rights, and continuing with various modern privacy laws and court decisions. Eleven states, for example, have passed laws protecting employees from being fired for smoking off the job.[1] Additionally, ten states have provisions in their constitutions regarding employee privacy.

Several areas of major concern regarding employee privacy are lack of security for personnel data, excessive zeal in collecting data, physical searches and electronic surveillance of employees, and employer policies regarding off-duty behavior, such as smoking.[2]

The Bill of Rights was designed to protect the citizen from oppression by the government, not from other citizens. This is why police officers have to "Mirandize" you — advise you of your rights — when they arrest you. Employers, private investigators, and security guards do not. No law requires them to do so. Freedom from government restrictions is the greatest advantage private investigation agencies have, and this more than compensates for lack of official police powers. Now let's look at specific laws purporting to protect your privacy.

At the federal level, the Privacy Act of 1974 bans sharing information gathered by different agencies in the Executive Branch of the federal government. In theory, this prohibits the FBI from tapping into the files of the IRS, but it doesn't quite work that way. There's a big difference between passing a law and enforcing it, and enforcement of the Privacy Act is the responsibility of the Executive Branch's Office of Management and Budget.[3] Today, sharing information is routine.

The same year, Congress authorized the Parent Locator Service. The purpose was to cull information from Social Security and tax records to locate parents who had skipped out on child support payments. However, the program hasn't worked quite as planned. Half of the requests processed are simply for absent parents who are not delinquent in payments.[4]

In theory, a court order is necessary for police officers to put a tap on your phone. This isn't any protection, because the system allows judges to issue these orders in secret. You may never get to know that a tap on your phone was ever authorized, unless it's introduced as evidence in your trial. In any case, modern technology has made the traditional wiretap, as we knew it, obsolete.

The Fair Credit Reporting Act provided that consumers were allowed to obtain a copy of their credit records at a small charge from credit bureaus. In practice, the charge runs between ten and twenty dollars. Now, there is a new push to tighten regulations governing credit bureaus, and to provide no-charge copies of credit reports to consumers. However, given the massive opposition that the big credit reporting organizations have been able to muster, the prospects of seeing a new law are shaky.[5]

The Foreign Bank Secrecy Act of 1970, despite its title, has nothing to do with protecting or enhancing the secrecy of your banking records. The Act is a misnomer, in the same sense that

"Right to Work" laws do not grant or guarantee anyone a job, but are merely laws to facilitate union-busting. The Bank Secrecy Act requires, among other things, that banks keep microfilm records of your checks for six years, for possible inspection by government agents. The act also spells out the conditions under which federal agents may dig into your financial affairs. These are the theoretical limitations.

In practice, both federal agents and local police often have access to your banking records. The usual practice is to cultivate a friendly relationship with a bank officer. This can begin with an offer to check out prospective employees with the criminal data files. In return, the bank officer helps the federal or police agent in his investigations by providing confidential information about accounts.

Sometimes the agents use pressure. The informal request is only the first step. If the bank officer doesn't comply, the agent can use a "pocket summons," a pre-signed blank subpoena which the agent fills out on the spot. The bank officer knows that it will save everyone time and money to provide the records upon demand, rather than trying to fight it in court. In any case, requests are often for official purposes, such as uncovering welfare cheats, tax dodgers, organized crime leaders, etc. Private detectives also obtain information from banks, using misrepresentation and bribes if necessary.[6]

Another important law is the Employee Polygraph Protection Act of 1988, which prohibits employers from requiring applicants to submit to polygraph examinations as a condition of employment. This is a fairly broad law, with some exceptions. It does not apply to many government agencies, and does not apply to local and state police. Other exceptions are private security firms and pharmaceutical manufacturers. If you want to work for any of these, you can still be required to submit to the polygraph.

An important point about privacy laws at all levels is that they're very limited, usually restricting the disclosure of information to authorized agencies. They usually don't cover "redisclosures," or second-hand disclosures. For example, a state law may allow a bank to release information about you to a credit bureau if you sign an authorization form. However, the credit bureau, once it has your information, can release it to anyone it chooses. Another problem has to do with state lines and jurisdiction limitations. Medical information, which you may consent for your doctor to release when you apply for health insurance, goes to the insurance company's home office, which is often in another state. It ultimately goes to the Medical Information Bureau, which serves as a clearing-house for member insurance companies, and is located in still another state. With data exchange between different computers, your records can be on file in several different places.

Today, it's possible to squirt data through a wire from one computer to another, using modems. Electronic data transmission doesn't observe national borders. This is why the law especially can't help you if your records are on file in another country. Canadian government officials were dismayed to find that financial records of many Canadian citizens were in computers in the United States. American Express, for example, has many Canadian customers, although it's a U.S. corporation. In another instance, discussed below, a right-wing organization in the United States used a computer bulletin board to bypass Canadian laws regarding the importation of politically objectionable literature.

Lawsuits

Both private individuals and government agencies have sued on privacy issues. Sibi Soroka filed a class-action suit against Target Stores, which required him to take a three-hour psychological test when he applied for employment. He stated that the questions, some of which centered around sex, politics, and religion, were too intrusive.

Attorneys General in several states have sued TRW for privacy invasion and dissemination of inaccurate information, based upon hundreds of customer complaints. States include Alabama, Arkansas, California, Delaware, Florida, Idaho, Louisiana, Michigan, Nevada, New Hampshire, New Mexico, New York, Pennsylvania, and Texas. According to New York State Attorney General Robert Abrams, TRW uses a secret scoring system of credit rating, which TRW deletes from consumers' copies of credit reports but provides to its business customers.[7]

December 1991 brought a resolution of the issues. TRW settled out of court, agreeing to make serious changes in the way it compiles and processes information. One day after TRW settled the lawsuits, it announced large cut-backs in its work force.[8] Whether this meant that TRW was divesting itself of faulty compilers or simply trimming fat was unclear.

A major problem with any lawsuit for invasion of privacy is that it often rakes up the information you're trying to protect. You can be sure that, if you ever sue an individual, newspaper, or corporation for invasion of your privacy, their lawyer will try to make it as uncomfortable for you on the witness stand as he can.[9]

Another problem related to lawsuits is known as "discovery." This is a question-and-answer process in which lawyers for opposing sides try to get to see the cards in the other party's hand. There are written "interrogatories," lists of questions you must answer under oath. There are also "depositions," verbal fishing expeditions, in which lawyers can ask you questions about topics only remotely related to the central issue. A malpractice suit, for example, will open you up to questioning about your entire medical history, every doctor you ever had, and other tangential information.

Yet another problem with lawsuits, and any court action, is that it produces public records. In a divorce, for example, the decree will list what each party got in the final settlement. Any burglar, marketer, or other snooper has access to these records, and can determine who has assets.

Court Decisions

There have been various laws passed regarding wiretapping, but court decisions generally have been in favor of telephone bugging. The Olmstead Decision of 1928, by the U.S. Supreme Court, established that wiretapping was not a violation of the Fourth Amendment. A later decision, Katz vs. United States, (389 U.S. 347) ruled that a warrant was required for wiretapping. The Federal Communications Act of 1934 bans interception or disclosure of interstate communications, but in practice it lacks teeth. It also doesn't cover communications within a state. The Omnibus Crime Control Act of 1968 allows wiretapping by the federal government in national security cases.

Electronic interception is often undetectable, especially when it involves portable and cellular phones. No matter how stringent the law, both police and private parties can still intercept communications without a warrant. The only practical limitations are that they mustn't be caught at it, and that they can't present the intercepts as evidence in court. However, they can use any information obtained as investigative leads. Some police officers, taking advantage of the latitude allowed by courts, will even list an intercept as a "confidential informant" in a search warrant affidavit.[10]

There have been many court decisions regarding the handling of criminal records. The Louisiana Supreme Court, in its 1906 Itzkovitch vs. Whitaker decision, ruled that police could not post the plaintiff's picture in the rogues' gallery because he had never been convicted. In 1944, a New Jersey court decision stated that, without a relevant law, police were empowered to destroy fingerprints, photographs, and records of those accused but not convicted. In 1966, the U.S. Court of Appeals ruled in the Herschel vs. Dyra case that, as there was no law covering the issue, police could keep arrest records on file, regardless of the disposition of the case.

The Menard vs. Mitchell Decision of 1971 allowed the FBI to retain records, and even to disclose them to private individuals for employment purposes. Menard then sued the Attorney General and won another decision, in 1974, to have his criminal records expunged, although the FBI was allowed to keep his fingerprints.

The 1979 Tatum vs. Rogers decision involved using computerized arrest records in setting bail for a person who had had many arrests, but few convictions. Obviously, providing arrest records without the subsequent dispositions biased the information, and Tatum won this case.

All of these decisions, and others not cited here because of space, affect only the official keeping and disclosure of records. Two technological developments have made all of these decisions moot.

One is the widespread use of the Xerox and other types of photocopy machines. Even if an ironclad decision comes down, requiring all police agencies to physically return all fingerprint cards of suspects arrested but not convicted, it's a simple matter to make a photocopy of each card before handing it over. The other is the widespread use of the computer.

Computer files are electronic records of anything from text, through fingerprints, to color photographs of arrested persons. Any computer file can be duplicated indefinitely, without practical limit to the number of copies made. Therefore, it's meaningless even to try to control or restrict computer record-keeping by police agencies and private parties. Once the information is on a disk, or passed to another computer via a modem, it's truly out of control. Handing back the original records, such as fingerprint cards and mug shots, is meaningless.

Another practical point is that, because of the delicacy of computer equipment, and the value of the records stored, computers are usually kept in secure environments. Access to the computer room is limited to authorized persons, and file retrieval is controlled. Rigid security measures limit remote access. It's practically impossible for a person, or his attorney, to physically search a government computer for his records. If you are ever arrested, acquitted, and released, you may get your arrest records back, but you've got no way of verifying that those are the only copies. In fact, the odds are overwhelming that there are duplicates somewhere.

Criminal records are not necessarily accurate, and they're certainly not secure. Although laws exist protecting the confidentiality of criminal records, they don't do any good if the violators are the police themselves. There have been several instances surfacing of police officials passing or selling criminal records to unauthorized parties.[11] This has created a strange situation in which law enforcement officials have concocted false criminal records for their undercover operatives because they knew that organized-crime elements had pipelines into police records.

In other cases, police and private agencies practice mutual back-scratching. Banks provide financial history information to police regarding persons under investigation. Police reciprocate by checking applicants for bank employment for criminal histories.

Bureaucratic Obstructionism

Bureaucrats don't like to be hampered by laws, especially if they're in the control business. There are several classes of tactics they use to circumvent the law, legislative intent, and public discussion.

The first is keeping a low profile, and not advertising exactly what they're doing. A favorite bureaucratic ploy is to go ahead and do something, in the absence of an explicit prohibition, instead of first asking permission. With luck, legislators will never find out what's actually happening.

The law usually does not protect against privacy intrusions because legislators can only pass laws against practices of which they're aware. Various government operations remain out of Congressional scrutiny, shielded by a complex organizational table and euphemistic names. A "statistical office" doesn't sound very interesting, but may be the cover for computerized surveillance of millions of citizens.

Another technique is disguising intent with euphemisms. When the FBI began its program to computerize its manual identification files, it did not identify this as a new program in its budget request to Congress. Instead, it passed it off as a "modernization" of an existing file system.[12]

FinCEN is a new database sponsored by several government agencies to exchange data without running afoul of the existing laws. Its 200 employees, recruited from the FBI, CIA, and other government agencies, simply collect as much information as they can, including financial and credit information. This is the beginning of a tremendous cross-matching capability, which will be accessible only to official agencies.[13]

Private Organizations

Another way around the law is to transfer the activity into a private organization, not under the scrutiny of legislators. The organization may be a private detective agency or an industry association. It may also be a central information clearing-house. A private organization does not have to report to Congress, or submit a budget for approval. This allows keeping a very low profile, and many of the people investigated won't even know it exists.

Private organizations are responsible only to themselves. They are not required to make public disclosures of every activity and function, and many remain behind closed doors. The International Association of Chiefs of Police set up its National Bureau of Criminal Identification as early as 1896. A loose association of law enforcement officers set up the Law Enforcement Intelligence Unit (LEIU) about 1960, to exchange information about organized crime.

Sometimes the purpose is good. The LEIU was a way of circumventing police forces, because many were infiltrated by organized crime. It takes only one crooked cop to leak information and nullify an entire investigative effort. The members of LEIU were very careful in accepting recruits, admitting only those sponsored by another member, to weed out possibly crooked cops.

It's easy to dismiss private police forces and organizations as being insignificant because they lack police powers. Members cannot make arrests, except for citizen's arrests, and they lack the power to request search warrants and subpoenas. Actually, they don't need them because they are free to act in ways official police cannot. Private police forces, while lacking police powers, are also free of the restrictions applied to police officers. Court decisions affecting criminal records, for example, don't apply to them because they're not police organizations.

Other private organizations have compiled criminal history databases in perfectly legal ways, such as by scanning publicly-available court records, abstracting newspaper stories, and using other public documents. They sell their services to landlords, banks, credit bureaus, and employers, as unofficial criminal history providers. Some credit bureaus regularly scan police and court records, as well as newspaper accounts, for information they can match to the names they have on file.

Credit reporting bureaus maintain massive files. The two largest, TRW and Equifax, each have about 150 million files on individual Americans.[14] However, an Associated Press estimate puts TRW's total at 170 million.[15] There were about 1,200 local credit reporting bureaus in this country a few years ago, and the number's been decreasing because of the absorption of smaller companies by the giants. Right now, late 1991, the number is about 450. Most of the smaller bureaus are subsidiaries of the "big three:" TRW, Equifax, and Trans Union.

Some private organizations keep track of people for bizarre reasons. One right-wing leader of the 1960s, Robert DePugh, advised his Minuteman followers to keep track of subversives by scrutinizing news accounts, as well as direct surveillance. If, for example, they suspected a certain college professor of having subversive leanings, they could build up a dossier on him by saving news clippings about speeches he made, organizational meetings he attended, and any public appearances reported in the media. Undercover agents posing as students might attend his classes, and write down any left-leaning or unpatriotic statements he made. Checking with the telephone and city directories would yield his address, and surveillance would provide the type and license number of his vehicle. The publication also advised Minutemen to record the target's likes, habits, weak and strong points, and physical description for future reference.[16]

At least two right-wing organizations today operate computer bulletin boards, serving as information networks for their members. One bulletin board was set up specifically to send messages into Canada, which has strict controls over importation of printed matter. The other bulletin board provides a database of enemies, including a list of addresses of Anti-Defamation League offices and names of civil-rights activists such as Morris Dees, head of the Southern Poverty Law Center.[17] The "Aryan Liberty Network" contained a list of "race traitors" and "informers," available to any member who logged on.[18] No doubt, the Anti-

Defamation League and the Southern Poverty Law Center maintain their own databases, as well.

Police have uncovered at least one network of pedophiles and child molesters who exchanged information using computer bulletin boards. They would "upload" accounts of their own affairs, and exchange names, addresses, and other personal data on children they considered attractive.

Evading The Laws

Unfortunately, laws are merely defensive tactics, and always a step behind law-breakers. In business, there are many clever ways of circumventing or evading laws or legal consequences. One well-known example is the "code." To avoid being sued by former employees for giving out derogatory information, employers have established a way to signal each other whether or not they consider an employee desirable. If they feel that the employee is desirable, and he left on good terms, they provide a glowing report, even on the telephone, to anyone who inquires. If they fired the employee, or he left under a cloud, they don't give any information over the phone, and state that any requests must be made in writing. They do not reply to the written request. This is the way they convey negative information without actually saying or writing anything that might incur liability.

The Bottom Line

Statutes and court decisions regarding electronic surveillance, record-keeping, and expunging of obsolete or inaccurate records are almost irrelevant because it's so easy to ignore or circumvent them. Many have no penalties, or such slight sanctions, that nobody bothers to obey them. In reality, enforcement of data privacy is almost non-existent, and violations take place literally every day. Both official and private police agencies do this routinely, but their agents are very rarely prosecuted for these transgressions. Technological advances have made the law itself obsolete.

Notes

1. *Smokers' Advocate,* June 1991, p. 6.

2. *Security Management,* June, 1991, p. 13.

3. *Dossier Society,* Kenneth C. Laudon, New York, Columbia University Press, 1986, pp. 5-6.

4. *Ibid.,* p. 329.

5. *Wall Street Journal,* October 25, 1991. Article by Michael W. Miller.

6. *Privacy in America,* David F. Linowes, Chicago, IL, University of Illinois Press, 1989, pp. 106-107.

7. *Consumer Reports,* November 1991, p. 710.

8. Associated Press, December 12, 1991.

9. *Low Profile,* William Petrocelli, New York, McGraw-Hill, 1981, pp. 125-126.

10. *No Place to Hide,* Alan LeMond and Ron Fry, New York, St. Martin's Press, 1975, pp. 7-8.

11. *Dossier Society,* pp. 92-94.

12. *Ibid.,* p. 62.

13. *How to Get Anything on Anybody, Book II,* Lee Lapin, San Mateo, CA, ISECO, Inc., 1991, p. 154.

14. *Time Magazine,* November 11, 1991, p. 37.

15. Associated Press, December 12, 1991.

16. *On Target,* February 1, 1964.

17. *Brotherhood of Murder*, Thomas Martinez and John Gunther, New York, Pocket Books, 1988, pp. 277-278.
18. *Privacy in America*, p. 20.

5

Who's Opening Your Mail?

Nominally, we have the First Amendment to protect the right of free speech, and by inference, the right to read what we wish. If we check out public library books, though, police may scrutinize the lists to see what we read. The same goes for any magazines to which we subscribe. Although the government and its agents cannot restrict our right to read what we wish, and to subscribe to any sort of publications we like, they use subscription lists as investigative tools. The Drug Enforcement Administration, for example, obtains leads to marijuana growers from subscriptions to *High Times*, a publication devoted to enjoyment of weed and other illegal substances.[1]

Both federal and local police have taken further steps against the publishers of *High Times*. Federal prosecutors began a flurry of grand jury subpoenas against the publication, seeking among other things, a list of all current and past employees. DEA officers have raided companies that advertise in the publication. North Carolina State Police raided a man's home without a warrant because he had ordered three light meters from a *High*

Times advertiser, but it turned out that the man was growing orchids.[2]

Many publications sell their subscription lists, and some investigative agencies avail themselves of the opportunity to obtain the names of people interested in the subject matter. The government isn't very interested in the subscriber list of *House and Garden*, but readers of more arcane publications are targets. Businesses often want lists of people with specialized interests as potential clients. In any case, owners of these publications know that some companies and agencies are willing to pay for their lists, and making money is the name of the game.

Not all publications are as cooperative, however, and some refuse to sell their lists to police agencies, or to anyone at all. In some cases, an undercover operative may obtain employment in the publication's office, but this extreme step isn't necessary. A "mail cover" can provide the names and addresses of subscribers.

The Mail Cover

The "mail cover" is a little-known investigative tool that the post office has been using since Day One. The mail cover is merely a listing of all addresses to which a party sends mail, or the return addresses of people writing to a certain party. As many people put return addresses on their envelopes, it's not necessary to violate the sanctity of first-class mail to identify the sender. In the case of publications, copying subscriber names and addresses from mailing labels is simple and routine.

The "Earth First!" case is instructive. Although Earth First! was careful to protect its members and subscribers, its leaders completely underestimated the diligence with which the government would come after them. They advised people writing to them to omit return addresses on their letters, and stated that they would burn all correspondence after reading it, to preclude a squad of government "plumbers" from obtaining the names by breaking and entering. This, of course, was not enough. A simple mail cover revealed names and addresses of all to whom they wrote, or sent copies of their book, *Ecodefense*.

Earth First! leaders were the victims of an FBI undercover operation which recruited an artist/sculptor from a small Arizona town to join the organization and report upon its activities. This person actually suggested certain acts of vandalism against power lines leading to the Palo Verde nuclear generating station, and when members of the group tried to carry them out, the FBI's S.W.A.T. Team was waiting for them.

Court-ordered Reading of Mail

Postal inspectors do not need a court order to start a mail cover on you. They do need one if they want to open your mail. As with telephone taps, these can be obtained secretly, and you may never know that postal inspectors are reading your mail. In practice, it can even happen without a court order, although the results cannot be used in evidence without the court order to "CYA" (Cover Your Ass).

Political Fringe Groups

Some political fringe groups, such as the "Posse Comitatus," that advertise for members attract spurious applicants who are really law enforcement officers.[3] This is part of the continuing process of low-grade surveillance of possible threats. Although you may feel that, if your conscience is clear you have nothing to fear, it's not that simple.

Answering an ad placed by a fringe group results in your name and address entered in the group's records. It's not necessary to join for your name to go on a list of prospects. If law officers ever have the occasion to "bust" the group and seize its records, your name will go into a police central file for possible correlation with other information. A simple loophole in the law allows this. The "exclusionary rule" mandates that any evidence obtained during service of a search warrant not stipulated in the affidavit cannot be used as evidence in a criminal prosecution. There is no such limitation regarding investigative leads, which usually do not serve as evidence, but merely point the way for further investigation. Investigative leads are much more dangerous than ordinary evidence, because there's no control over them and they can point to legally admissible evidence.

Notes

1. *Law Enforcement News*, July/August 1991.
2. *The Drug Policy Letter*, May/June 1991, p. 9.
3. *How to Use Mail Drops For Fun and Profit*, Jack Luger, Port Townsend, WA, Loompanics Unlimited, 1988, p. 40.

6

IRS Cross-Matching Programs

Originally, very few Americans were subject to the income tax. Today, the government's voracious appetite for money has made practically all Americans liable for the federal tax bite. This is why the Internal Revenue Service has pushed electronic data processing vigorously.

One day soon, the IRS will have all functions computerized. A main function will be to match all Form 1099s, reports of payments, to the proper tax returns. Right now, the volume of Form 1099s, used to report interest and dividend payments as well as contract labor, is too great to allow complete matching, and most end up in shredders and furnaces because the IRS lacks the manpower to match them manually. Individual tax filers can still under-report their incomes, with a better than even chance that the IRS won't be able to pull enough records together to prove them wrong. Once 1099 computerized matching is in force, nobody will be able to escape having all of his income reported.

Today, electronic tax return filing is practical. You can send your return in over the wire with a modem, which is an advantage if you're getting a refund and want to expedite the process.

One problem with tax returns is that they're not truly confidential. Tax returns were public record until the Tax Reform Act of 1976 closed some routes of access. Today, it's not possible for a casual snooper to walk in and scrutinize your finances. However, only casual snoopers are truly excluded.

Although the IRS Code prohibits casual disclosure, there are loopholes. There are at least 29 exceptions, such as state and local tax agencies. We can say that these have a legitimate reason for wanting to know how much you earn. They want to collect their fair share of taxes from you as well. However, there is no way to control what state and local agencies do with information the IRS provides. Even other federal agencies, constrained by the "redisclosure" rule, are not effectively policed to ensure that they don't pass on your personal information.

The net effect of enhanced government computer power has been many "matching" programs, some using IRS information. The Justice Department, Health and Human Services Department, and the Social Security Administration receive information from the IRS. In practice, your tax return can be used against you if you're delinquent in making child support payments, and your refund check is open to seizure because the IRS cooperates with the Parent Locator Service. You can also be denied benefits from various government programs on the basis of information from the IRS, although you have the right to challenge that information.

Computer matching of tax and employee records with welfare payment records can uncover welfare cheats, and matching has been taking place since 1977. Today, front-end matching is the rule. Your income will be verified before you can obtain unemployment or welfare benefits.[1]

Another application has been to find draft dodgers, possibly a redundancy because there hasn't been a draft for years. The Selective Service System is a dinosaur, but it still exists, although the likelihood of our country needing mass armies is practically nil in today's technological warfare age. However, the Selective Service System is comparing lists of taxpayers with birth records to detect those who have survived to draft age and are working.[2] Birth records by themselves aren't very useful because of the number of people who die during childhood, or become disabled, etc. However, those able-bodied enough to hold jobs are of definite interest to the Selective Service System.

The Selective Service System has also bought a list of 18-year-olds from Farrel's, a chain of ice cream parlors that operates a birthday club. Applicants fill out cards with their names, addresses, and ages, and receive a free ice cream on each birthday, and their names go into Farrel's data bank.[3]

The General Accounting Office conducted a cross-matching program to uncover veterans who had filed fraudulent claims. This involved checking Internal Revenue Service records against the benefit rolls of the Department of Veterans Affairs. There had been discrepancies between income some veterans declared to the IRS and income figures supplied in their applications for benefits. About 116,000 veterans had failed to disclose income from savings account interest, stock dividends, or rents, and had collected $338 million in fraudulent benefits in 1989. About 13,600 veterans had understated their true incomes by at least $4,000, while 5,500 had fudged the figures by $10,000 or more on their pension applications. One outstanding individual under-reported his income by over $300,000. There will be another cross-matching run against Social Security Administration records to uncover frauds and duplications.[4]

The IRS wants to know everything it can find out about your finances, for obvious reasons. The IRS also has a hidden agenda, though. This is universal registration.

Notes

1. *Privacy in America*, David F. Linowes, Chicago, IL, University of Illinois Press, 1989, pp. 92-93.

2. *Ibid.*, p. 93.

3. *Wall Street Journal*, March 14, 1991. Article by Michael W. Miller.

4. *Los Angeles Times*, December 25, 1991.

7

Universal Registration

Universal registration is a concept foreign to Americans. Most European countries have universal registration of all people within their borders, including citizens and aliens. Some are repressive regimes, while others, such as France and Sweden, are typical liberal European socialist countries.

Sweden began its current system of national registration on January 1, 1947, providing each person living in Sweden with a Person-Number, or "PN." The central record has been computerized since 1967. Each person's record includes name, number, birthdate, place of birth, church registration locality, and address. The record also includes marital status, including dates, citizenship, legal status, and membership or non-membership in the official state religion, the Church of Sweden. It also contains information on pension status, draft status, merchant navy register, and income tax information. All of this falls under the authority of, and is operated by, the National Tax Board.

This comprehensive identity system serves many purposes, according to the Swedish Government. As a start, it serves to register the population, making the census-taker's job much easier. The Tax Board also uses it to ensure it collects its share of the person's income. The draft board keeps track of all eligible persons, as does Civil Defense. It also serves as an identifier for education, as well as social and health insurance. The National Police Board also keeps track of passport applicants through their PNs.

Health statistics are an important part of the Swedish government's population tracking system, and the PN enables close monitoring of epidemics, cancer data, and the side-effects of drugs.[1]

In Sweden, the registering authority is the National Tax Board. It's significant that the U.S. agency most concerned with developing a national identity system is the Treasury Department. It has taken over a lot of the data regarding persons with Social Security Numbers, and uses this as a taxpayer identifier. With new regulations requiring children to have Social Security numbers to make them tax-deductible, it's taken a giant step toward universal registration of the population.

Government bureaucrats want total control, and they are aided in this by overzealous police officers, who see universal registration as a crime-fighting tool. Some police officers have for years been demanding that all babies be fingerprinted at birth, as a permanent identifier, to enable the government to track citizens throughout their lives. A congressional report on the "SUI," or Single Universal Identifier, attracted attention during the last decade, but Congress rejected the idea. No legislation requiring such fingerprinting has ever passed in any state, but police officials have managed to get many children fingerprinted through a back door approach.

Traditionally, only lawbreakers were required to be finger-printed. World War II brought about a new set of programs. Anyone inducted into the armed forces got fingerprinted, as did many civilians. Many persons working in defense-related industries had to apply for security clearances as a condition of employment, and each applicant had to furnish two fingerprint cards to the Defense Industrial Security Clearance Office. DISCO checked applicants out with the FBI by providing the FBI with a fingerprint card. The FBI, of course, filed it away.

The 1980s saw a media-inspired hysteria over child abuse, and police officials were quick to turn the situation to their advantage. While many credulous parents panicked and expected their children to be kidnaped by child murderers, police officials urged fingerprinting, presumably to help identify the bodies. Police officers, aided by volunteers and a slick public relations campaign, set up fingerprinting booths at shopping centers, fairs, and other public events. Millions of children were brought for fingerprinting by their parents, and their prints went into a computerized file. Needless to say, these files never get erased. Today, the FBI files hold about 200 million sets of fingerprints. Criminal files are only a small fraction of this number.

This isn't enough for Big Brother. Bureaucrats would like to see every citizen carry a national identity card, as is the practice in some European countries. Congress has to date rejected this, but universal registration has nevertheless slipped in through the back door. Parents must now apply for a Social Security number for each child over one year old they claim as a deduction. Many states' drivers licenses now use the Social Security number instead of a state-generated code number. The armed forces no longer provide numbers for personnel, because their serial numbers are their Social Security numbers. In effect, the Social Security number has become the American Universal Identifier. In practice, the drivers license has become the national identity card. Some people who don't drive now apply for "non-drivers licenses" for check-cashing, because all American drivers licenses are now photographic, and generally accepted as I.D. documents.

Notes

1. *Understanding U.S. Identity Documents*, John Q. Newman, Port Townsend, WA, Loompanics Unlimited, 1991, pp. 19-31.

8

Eye in the Sky

Some police agencies operate their own air forces, using helicopters and light fixed-wing aircraft for rescue operations, medical evacuation, and of course, aerial surveillance. One type of aerial surveillance which has become popular during the 1980s is marijuana interdiction.

Marijuana leaves have a distinctive color, a shade of Kelly green, and this stands out from most surrounding foliage. Aerial surveillance usually takes a crew of two: a pilot and an observer, usually a nark officer, to watch the landscape. Sometimes, gyro-stabilized binoculars help the effort, and a camera loaded with color film is necessary for supporting photographs.[1]

Airborne narks follow several leads in searching for illicit marijuana "gardens." First is "information received" from snitches. A snitch may be a competitor using the police to put his rival out of business. He may also be informing for pay, or to work a "deal" on a criminal charge.

Narks also know that a marijuana garden requires lots of water, and gardens are usually located near a river or stream, or where piped water is available. Sunlight is a must, and the garden must be open to view. Some growers shield their gardens with a hothouse, and the translucent plastic cover frustrates airborne narks.

The ideal marijuana garden is in a remote area, with a nearby source of water, and is accessible by road. Airborne narks keep a watch on as many of these locations as they can, but there are too many to watch constantly. Some growers plant in remote locations, and leave the gardens unattended, to minimize the risk. They pick locations visible from a long way off, so that they can spot if any narks are staking out their gardens when they return.

There is some danger in spotting marijuana gardens from the air. In Northern California, airborne narks have drawn gunfire when cruising over marijuana gardens, and even pilots of light aircraft unconnected with law enforcement have reported being taken under fire.

Ultralights

Some police departments, such as Monterey Park, California, and Tempe, Arizona, for a while employed ultralight aircraft for aerial surveillance. Single-occupant ultralights were helpful in observing traffic patterns, following escaping suspects, and spotting some crimes in progress. With their relatively quiet engines and small propellers, they were truly low-tech "stealth" vehicles for police surveillance. Police agencies steadfastly denied that they were used to spot skinny-dippers, but some residents looked up at the sky nervously when preparing to swim in the buff in their own pools.

There was some reason for anxiety, although not over skinny-dipping. Police did use the ultralights to spot unlicensed home modifications, and the residents soon received visits from the city's building inspectors.

A new development, advertised in law enforcement magazines, is the remote piloted drone, or RPD. One type, manufactured by Aerovironment, Inc., of Simi Valley, California, was originally developed for the U.S. Marine Corps for military surveillance. The system uses a stealth model airplane, powered by an electric motor and lithium battery, for silent operation at low altitude. The craft itself is six feet long, with a nine-foot wingspan, and weighs eight pounds, including a payload of a black & white or color TV camera and transmitter.

This system is designed for discreet, quiet surveillance of distant suspect locations, and even pursuit of vehicles not exceeding 50 mph. An optional night vision sensor allows viewing a scene by extremely low light, using an electronic light amplification tube. The low operating altitude, 300-500 feet, and slow speed, permit clear pictures, transmitted to a ground station for real-time viewing.

Commercial Aerial Photography

Some police agencies routinely purchase aerial photographs of their jurisdictions. These are produced by commercial aerial survey companies, and show streets and individual buildings. Large-scale photographs show small details, such as fences, bushes, and other features.

One application for such photographs is to disclose those who have made home improvements without obtaining the required licenses and building permits. Police S.W.A.T. teams keep files of aerial photographs to provide information on the layout and surroundings of any building they may have to besiege.

Notes:

1. "Anatomy of a Marijuana Raid," *Arizona Highway Patrolman*, January, 1985.

9

Surveillance of Businesses

The United States Secret Service, in its efforts to prevent counterfeiting, has operated a low-key program of business surveillance for many decades. Secret Service agents maintain liaison with printing equipment suppliers, ink and paper manufacturers, and graphic arts dealers, to find out who is ordering materials useful for counterfeiting currency. Certain paper stocks, which resemble the government's exclusive stock used for currency, are on a special watch list. So are inks in the shades used for printing money.

Aerial surveillance by drug agents has led to increased efforts to grow pot indoors. The DEA keeps an eye on suppliers of high-tech gardening materials and equipment. Hydroponic suppliers are in for special scrutiny, because this equipment allows growing marijuana indoors, completely out of sight of prowling aircraft and other visual surveillance. In some cases, DEA agents have used "administrative subpoenas" to require suppliers to hand over documents, sales receipts, shipping records, correspondence, and even employee records. In 1989, DEA agents raided gardening suppliers, and obtained search warrants for some of their customers. Some judges, especially in Missouri, upheld the seizures because DEA agents had obtained supporting information, such as evidence of unusually high electricity consumption and a subscription to *High Times*.[1]

Various government agencies, such as the Securities and Exchange Commission, track the financial activities of many companies to seek out illegalities such as "insider trading." The stock market is, of course, under constant surveillance, with easy access because today it's operated by computer. This allows regulators to zero in on anyone trading in stocks and bonds and list his transactions.

Notes

1. *Law Enforcement News*, July/August, 1991.

10

Modern Electronic Surveillance

Today, almost everybody knows that wiretapping is common, and career criminals watch what they say during telephone conversations. When they have to use the phone, they speak in circumlocutions and guarded terms, to make it as hard as possible for an eavesdropper to understand.

Some people, however, never learn, and others are incredibly careless. One drug dealer used his portable telephone to negotiate his drug deals, not realizing that his voice was audible to anyone within range on the same channel. A neighbor informed the police, and officers began listening in during his incriminating conversations. This technique, used to gather evidence, was upheld by the court.

If a police officer wants to tap your line, he no longer needs to climb up on a telephone pole outside your home and physically attach wires to your line. Modern electronic switching systems (ESS) and computerized call directing make it possible to monitor calls from a central location, just by pushing a few buttons on a control panel. Police officers normally work closely with phone company security officers, who themselves are often retired police officers, FBI agents, etc., making them part of the "old boy network." Likewise, many private investigators are retired law enforcement officers, and they maintain their contacts with their colleagues who have gone to work for the phone company.

The real threats to privacy are not from electronic eavesdropping, but from electronic data processing. Electronic passcards, originally devised as alternatives to keyed locks, can now be used to monitor your movements within a restricted area. Credit cards, bank cards and cash machine cards all leave electronic trails. Government agents and private parties can keep an electronic file on you and trace your life, work history, hobbies, finances, and almost everything worth knowing about you. While the law requires a court order to tap your line, most other information about you is available through electronic means without any legal formalities at all.

If you're in the habit of paying for everything by check, you leave a paper trail behind you. If you pay with credit or debit cards, you leave both a paper and electronic trail, which makes tracking your movements very easy for anyone with access to your records.

Credit cards, such as Mastercard, American Express, and Diner's Club, are a fact of life today because many people use them. Point-of-sale cards, which debit your bank account the moment you pay for anything with them, also create electronic records of transactions. One use of credit card purchase records is to estimate your income. Using profiles derived from interviewing representative samples of Americans, plus the financial information some people provide freely about themselves if they fill out warranty forms completely, credit bureaus can correlate credit card spending with income level.

Your credit card use allows an investigator to track your movements. Police make direct use of this information. One case involved the shooting of a police officer outside a New York restaurant. Investigators were unable to find any witnesses, but they contacted American Express. Half a day later, they had a list of 20 persons who had paid with American Express cards in that restaurant that night. Investigators interviewed these people, and were able to solve the case.[1]

In one recent case, police followed a credit card trail in an effort to find a resident of Camp Verde, Arizona, who had apparently been abducted. John Calvin Anderson had been missing since December 5, 1991, last seen at a tire store in Phoenix. A cash withdrawal was recorded at a bank automatic teller machine 45 minutes later. A witness saw Anderson's car on an interstate highway, with the driver signaling with a windshield screen saying HELP, CALL POLICE. Credit card receipts and ATM records placed Anderson, or someone using his cards, at Phoenix, Chandler, Tucson, Blythe, Los Angeles, and San Diego. At a Phoenix bank, an ATM camera photographed a blond woman trying to use Anderon's card, and police were able to identify her. The car was found in a supermarket parking lot on December 15th.[2]

Computer Matching

The federal government has a program of matching names on various lists to identify those who are defrauding it in various areas, such as welfare. State agencies followed suit. One type of match is to compare names on employee lists with those receiving welfare or unemployment benefits, to discover cheaters. This was the main theme of programs begun during the 1970s. Today, with larger data banks and faster computers, "front-end" matching is the trend, with an electronic records search whenever a person applies for benefits.[3]

There have been many types of matching programs run. One was a comparison of IRS records and addresses with a list of birth records to find those who did not register with the Selective Service System. Comparing with birth records alone would not be very helpful, because some individuals died in childhood, became incapacitated, or left the country.

The City of New York, which has had a city income tax for several decades, is using a list of taxpayers from the IRS to identify those who are paying federal taxes but not city income taxes.

Another type of cross-matching run is the "National Driver Register." This came about because some drivers were obtaining licenses in nearby states after their home state licenses had been revoked. Originally, this caused no problem for the issuing state, because the non-resident driver's bad driving record did not concern them. However, a gradual awareness that bad drivers are everywhere led most states to join to close this loophole. Today, anyone applying for a drivers license in any state except Alaska, Florida, Montana, Nebraska and Rhode Island, gets checked through the NDR.[4]

Telephone Usage Patterns

Keeping track of telephone numbers, the electronic equivalent of the mail cover, is one way of ferreting out a target's friends and associates. The telephone often provides a very visible link between members of organized gangs. A device known as a "pen register" records the dial clicks of outgoing calls. A tape recorder does the same for touch-tone telephones. However, these devices aren't necessary any more, because the telephone company willingly provides records to police and private investigators.

Contrary to what some may think, telephone records aren't sacrosanct. While in theory a court order is necessary to tap a line, government agents who want to recover someone's telephone bills have only to ask their contact in the telephone company. This is usually the company security officer. A little-known fact is that telephone company security officers keep close liaison with police agencies of all types, and rarely refuse any requests. One important reason for this is that they are often retired police officers themselves, and part of the old boy network. Other retired officers employed by private security companies often enjoy the same privileges.

In June, 1991, Proctor & Gamble executives realized that someone in their company had leaked information to a reporter. The company had Cincinnati Bell scrutinize the long-distance records of 655,000 subscribers in the 513 and 606 area codes to see who had called the reporter's number in Washington.

Prescription Patterns

Narks are interested in people with legitimate uses for drugs, as well as illegal producers and dealers. Medical doctors come in for scrutiny, because some of them are "Doctor Feelgoods." This is the term for a doctor who will write a prescription for a mind-altering drug on patient demand. A Doctor Feelgood can earn quick fees because he doesn't need to examine a patient or puzzle out a diagnosis. He simply writes "scrip" for the drug of the patient's choice, pockets his fee, and awaits the next patient. This sort of supermarket medicine can be intensely profitable.

Drug enforcement agents seek out Doctor Feelgoods by scrutinizing prescription patterns. Agents regularly visit pharmacies and examine prescription records. Pharmacies with computerized prescription records, such as the larger chains, are fertile hunting grounds for two reasons:

1. They have an abundance of data, records of literally millions of prescriptions, to make agents' efforts worthwhile.

2. Their records are accessible electronically, making it unnecessary to scan each prescription record by eye.

Scanning prescription records allows drug enforcement agents to establish averages, or norms, for prescriptions of various drugs. It quickly becomes clear that the average number of prescriptions for product "X" is a certain number, and any doctors who exceed the average earn special scrutiny. Agents also look for patterns in prescribing. They know that doctors prescribe antibiotics, tranquilizers, hormones, painkillers, and other categories of drugs. Doctors who seem to specialize in painkillers and mind-altering drugs, while prescribing very few other types, show a pattern of guilt in their own handwriting.

Demographic Data

Demographic information is very valuable to marketers, who try to match their advertisements to the buying power and interests of customers. TV advertisers want to know what types of people watch shows they sponsor, in order to select shows that attract potential customers. One obvious connection is advertising beer during sporting events. Direct mail marketers also are acutely interested in the demographics of their mailing lists. They don't want to waste time, materials, and postage mailing advertisements to people who can't afford, or aren't interested in their products. An obvious example is advertising lawnmowers to people who actually own their houses, not apartment dwellers. Consumers Marketing Rescarch has provided lists of Japanese men for Brooks Brothers, who sought a list of buyers for its smaller sizes.[5]

Another use of demographics is to estimate credit risks. Believe it or not, today one of the factors deciding whether or not you get a loan is your ZIP code, because experience has shown that, on the average, residents of certain areas are better credit risks than others. This isn't a startling revelation, but using ZIP codes, especially now that the post office has refined them to the nine-digit ZIP + four numbers, is more precise than naming a city or neighborhood.

Fingerprints

Since fingerprints began to see use in criminal identification during the 1890s, police agencies have come to depend very much on them. Today, anyone arrested is fingerprinted, and periodically there are campaigns to fingerprint citizens who have committed no crimes. Today, all members of the armed forces are fingerprinted, as well as all civilian government employees. Anyone who applies for a security clearance related to work in the defense industries has to furnish a set of fingerprints. Applicants for various sorts of licenses, such as private investigators, also have to submit their prints. Some private companies require fingerprinting of all employees.

AFIS, or Automated Fingerprint Identification System, has been in existence for only about a decade, and at first only a few major police agencies used it. Today, with sharp declines in computer prices, AFIS is becoming more affordable for medium-size agencies.

What is AFIS and what purpose does it serve? Fingerprints are unique to each individual, and finding a person's prints at a crime scene is evidence that he or she was there. However, to make fingerprint comparisons, it's necessary to have both a questioned fingerprint, and a sample for comparison. Human fingerprint patterns vary a great deal, which makes them both extremely reliable as identifiers, and extremely difficult to compare. There are 64 billion possible combinations, and while there are systems of fingerprint classification, each category in each system is so broad that trying to find a certain fingerprint in a file containing thousands or millions of sets is practically impossible. Up to now, manual comparison by a trained fingerprint technician was the only way, and manpower limitations made it impractical to search the files for each crime case.

AFIS makes it speedy. The AFIS systems (there are several manufacturers) scan each fingerprint entered to reduce the pattern to a mathematical formula. A suspect fingerprint also becomes a mathematical formula, and the computer can compare it with millions of stored formulas in minutes. This isn't merely an improvement in performance, but a quantum jump, changing the entire complexion of forensic science. In California, the new computerized fingerprint system took only 90 seconds to find a match for a fingerprint left at the scene in the "Night Stalker" case.[6]

A major point for police is that criminals tend to be repeaters. Major cases often trace back to arrests for minor offenses earlier in criminals' careers. This makes a good case for fingerprinting everyone arrested, and keeping the prints on file. To be starkly realistic, most of those arrested are guilty, but the police can't prove it to the satisfaction of a court, which is why many get away. Keeping the prints on file can enable linking these early arrestees to a crime scene later in their careers.

In principle, at least, criminal cases result in fingerprint checks only against files of known criminals. Electronic data processing, with its blinding speed, makes it possible to compare a fingerprint against civilian files, as well.

Previously, only the most important cases rated extensive effort in making comparisons. In a murder case, latent prints at the scene would be compared with prints from the principal suspects. Today, prints from even marginal cases are subject to mass comparison. Fingerprints found on a letter to a crime suspect may go into the computer to see to who they belong to. Victims' fingerprints can be compared to those in a national file, as a special check for a criminal record or outstanding warrants.

Patterns and Constellations

Police agencies thrive on records, and many police forces, both in democratic countries and totalitarian regimes, owe their successes to the comprehensiveness of their files. In the modern era, the first national dossier system was devised by Joseph Fouche, a French police official of the early 19th century, to keep track of political radicals and extremists. This was for domestic security more than criminal surveillance, but it set the pattern for other police forces to emulate.[7]

Britain's national criminal police directorate, Scotland Yard, started a fingerprint filing system before the turn of the century. The Europeanization of America continued, with the International Association of Chiefs of Police instituting their National Bureau of Criminal Identification in 1896.[8]

This effort was unofficial. The IACP, despite its name, is a private organization composed mainly of American police chiefs, with a few Canadians and Mexicans included. It is privately funded by fees collected from members. Police executives often have their membership fees reimbursed by the parent body, the city or state which employs them, so indirectly the IACP is taxpayer-funded. In practice, it's accountable only to itself.

In 1923, the U.S. Department of Justice began quietly to merge the IACP files with those of the federal prison system. This enhanced the size and comprehensiveness of the files. The FBI accelerated its development of a national criminal records system during the 1930s, taking advantage of the depression-era hysteria over petty hoods and gangsters.

The Computer Revolution

Electronic data processing allows keeping extremely detailed and comprehensive records on everyone in the country. Police investigators thrive on lists, and any method of generating lists is welcome because it can lead to possible suspects.

Figure 10-1

This Mobile Data Terminal enables the officer to run a drivers license and vehicle registration check from his car, getting a reply within a minute or two.

An example is the search for a suspect in a child molesting. Without a good suspect description or other strong identifying data, police have to rely on other leads. A computer run can provide a list of all adult males in a certain locale who subscribe to sexually-oriented publications. Closer examination of the list reveals which publications contain material interesting to a potential child molester. Generating another list, this time of telephone calls to other child molesters around the country, can narrow the field even more. Finally, a list of those who answered decoy ads offering child-oriented material can shrink the field to just a few names of most likely suspects. A police agency can direct its investigative effort against those few names, and have a good chance of uncovering evidence.

Figure 10-2

The police dispatcher services officers on the road via CAD, Computer-Aided Dispatch. This provides information about addresses of calls, and a history of previous calls to each address listed. Other information is also available, depending on the agency and the type of equipment.

Today, patrol officers in even medium-size police agencies have mobile data terminals (MDTs) in their vehicles. These operate in the microwave band, making interception very difficult, unlike police radio vulnerable to scanners. Mobile computer terminals allow a patrol officer to run your name, drivers license, and plate number through state and national computers to check whether your drivers license is up to date, whether the vehicle is actually registered to you, and whether you're wanted for crimes. The computer will also tell the officer if your vehicle is on the stolen list. Depending on the agency, other information may be accessible through the MDT.

Figure 10-3

The computer room in a medium-size police agency. These banks of equipment record all radio and telephone calls, store information about each call and official action taken, and provide other information officers may need.

Private Computer Power

If you wanted to keep a computerized file of names and addresses before 1980, it was necessary to buy a small machine with limited capacity, and to write your own program to store, recall, and print out your list. It was much easier and much cheaper to keep a file of index cards. By the middle of the decade, many "database" programs were on the market. These allowed creating files configured to your own special needs, following simple instructions. Database programs allowed generating an electronic file card for each entry, listing a number of "fields," devoted to each type of information. A file with ten fields might list a person's first name, last name, street address, city, state, ZIP code, telephone number, religion, political affiliation, and reserve the last field for comments.

Most database programs are more sophisticated than this. They allow you to sort and categorize the entries by several categories, and even draw relationships between various entries. These advanced features are what require computing power. The original PC might take two hours to draw up a list of subscribers to *Time Magazine* who are also members of the Republican Party. A modern "486" machine can do this in a few minutes.

It's hard to lay down strict rules regarding exactly how many names can be stored in a particular computer memory, because this depends greatly on the size of each entry and its configuration. A list of names and addresses is very simple, and it's easy to store a million on a hard drive of moderate size. If your purpose is to list not only names and addresses, but many other bits of information about each person, plus a two-page biography, the total you'll be able to store on a particular drive will be much smaller. Also, the more sophisticated database programs have "compacting" or "squeezing" features, which remove unused space within each entry, freeing it for additional entries.

For many private users, the main value of a desk-top computer is not what it can store from its keyboard, but the access it provides to commercially-available databases. For this, it's necessary to gain access to data suppliers via telephone lines. Transmission of electronic data is cheap and easy. A modest modem, a device which squirts computer data over telephone lines, is available for well under $100. Upgrade models may cost two or three times that much, allowing a higher rate of data transmission. The practical value of higher-rate modems is to cut telephone and on-line bills.

COMPUSERVE is a well-known commercial computer service that allows access to a variety of databases. Some of these are medical and news databases, which allow the user to call up all entries on a particular subject, or entries containing a key word or phrase. These databases are electronic substitutes for poring through newspaper morgues.

DIALOG is another database service which allows access to over 600 individual databases, some of which contain unlisted telephone numbers.

DATATIMES is a news service database that picks up items from more than 30 regional newspapers.

EASYNET/TELEBASE SYSTEMS, INC. is a conglomerate offering access to about 1,000 databases. This company also provides hard copy upon demand.

VU/TEXT INFORMATION SERVICES, INC., provides a range of services similar to DIALOG.

WESTERN UNION INFOMASTER allows access to about 800 databases, including DIALOG, VU/NET, and others.

U.S. DATALINK is a specialized concern that can provide information from public documents in all 50 states. With this, it's possible to conduct an electronic search for someone, beginning with his name. With a common name, such as "Smith," it's wise to include more information, such as a social security or telephone number, to narrow the search. PC PROFILE is one of its databases, and provides information on criminal history, driving record, and comprehensive employment data. Another is PC AUTO, which traces a subject by his license plate.

NCI, "National Credit Information Network," sells personal information abstracted from credit bureau reports. While federal law prohibits selling credit reports for other than legitimate credit reporting purposes, a loophole in the law allows selling "headers," the personal information at the top of the report. This includes name, address, telephone number, family information, and any other information not specifically dealing with credit performance. NCI also sells the Post Office's forwarding address database, as well as a special reverse telephone directory that furnishes the nearest names and addresses of a given number.[9]

This short listing and accompanying descriptions provide a good overview of the many private information databases available to both private and public (official) investigators. One way or another, information about you is on file somewhere, and available to anyone who knows how to look for it.

Access Control and its Future

In sophisticated companies, key and combination locks to control who comes in and leaves are obsolete. For the last few decades, various forms of electronic locks have gradually taken their place. Push-button combination locks, with the combinations changed periodically for security, are only a primitive form of access control. Card-keys, with a magnetic stripe that identifies the user when passed through a reading slot, allow much more flexibility and control.

Figure 10-4

A quarter and a dime show the relative sizes of these miniature TV cameras. Some have wide-angle lenses for area surveillance, while others have remotely-controlled zoom lenses. Some have "pin-hole" adapters, allowing surveillance through tiny apertures in walls and ceilings.

A card-key is a plastic card with magnetically recorded data unique to you. Passing the card through a reading slot tells the electronic lock that you are legitimately allowed access. Combine it with a computer, linking all of the card readers in a facility, and the possibilities for surveillance greatly increase. The computer records every use of the card, so that it's no longer necessary to punch a time-card for your employer to know the exact moment you entered and left. The computer also prevents "pass-back," where you slip your card to someone else from a window or under the door once you're inside. When the computer records your entry, your card can no longer serve for entry until you leave. This helps keep unwanted people out of company parking lots, for example.

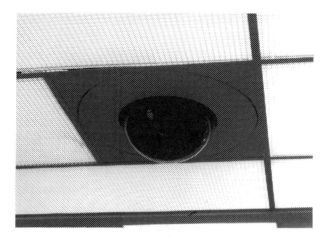

Figure 10-5

This smoked plastic dome, hanging down from the ceiling, contains a CCTV camera, remotely controlled to pan in all directions. Sophisticated models also have zoom lenses, allowing close inspection of everything a customer does. Significantly, camera domes are also located over check-out stands, where security officers can peer over the shoulders of clerks operating cash registers.

The computer, by reading your card and comparing it to its own memory, knows which areas of the facility you're authorized to enter. Unless you've been "cleared," it won't allow you access to restricted or secret areas. The computer also records each attempt at unauthorized use. If you try to enter a restricted area without authorization, the computer will record it when it denies you access, and you'll hear about it from the security department or your supervisor.

The "proximity card," first introduced in 1973, is a card that operates by reflecting or repeating a radio signal. The more sophisticated ones have their own lithium batteries, which last for years. With a proximity card, you don't need to slip the card itself into a slot. Simply carrying it on your person is enough, because its response to the radio signal put out by an electronically controlled door or gate is enough to open it, provided you're authorized. That's not the end of it, though. Sensors built into walls can track you everywhere you go within a controlled facility. This is called "passive monitoring," and is an electronic leash to keep you under control.[10]

Facilities with public access, such as retail stores, have other means of electronic surveillance. These often use CCTV, closed-circuit television, to monitor movements of both customers and employees.

Figure 10-6

This is a split-screen monitor, to allow viewing through four cameras at once. If the operator sees anything interesting in one view, he can expand it to fill the screen by flipping a switch. This allows constant monitoring of many remote areas, including the store's exterior, a corner of which is visible in the upper left frame.

To retailers, shoplifting is a serious cause of "stock shrinkage," the euphemistic term for loss by theft. Employee theft, however, is more common, and contains less risk, because employees know store security systems and the security officers operating them. This is why newer systems are specially designed to surveil employees and customers alike. For public-relations reasons, CCTV systems do not cover toilets, but we have only the retailers' word for this.

The most sophisticated installations are remotely-controlled, with a central control room located away from the main walkways in the store. The door to the control room isn't easily visible from inside the store, so that employees find it hard to determine if the control room is manned at a particular moment. This is the idea, as employers want their employees to feel slightly paranoid, potentially under surveillance through their entire shifts.

Inefficiencies

The computer revolution appears very sinister in potential, but it's also vulnerable to a surprising array of problems. It doesn't matter whether the effort is public or private, errors and inefficiencies creep into the process.

Do government computers speak to each other? In principle, yes, but there are problems. The government has been using computers since they were invented, and many of the older models, such as those produced during the 1960s and 1970s, use obsolete formats and languages. Recently, there have been problems reading stored data, because it's gibberish to modern computers. People who understood the old programs have retired, and stored information is unreadable.

Another problem that has surfaced is bad information. With computers, the governing principle is "GIGO," Garbage In, Garbage Out. A classic example of this showed up in Phoenix, Arizona, several years ago. A man reporting a burglary to the police was dismayed to find that, when the officer who came to take the report entered his name in his Mobile Data Terminal, the screen flashed the notation: "High Risk: AIDS." He and a number of other residents of the area were listed in the central computer, shared by the Phoenix Police Department and the Maricopa County Sheriff's Office, as AIDS risks for reasons which seemed insubstantial. In his case, he had been at a gathering in a Phoenix city park when police took down the license plate of his vehicle. The reason was that the gathering included many homosexuals, and officers presumed that these were high AIDS risks. In fact, this man had never taken a test for AIDS, and did not even know if he had the disease.[11]

The implications of this case are both frightening and funny. The newspaper account did not state whether the man was, in fact, homosexual. His presence at a party or gathering frequented by homosexuals is thin evidence, and as an indication of infection by AIDS, is very unreliable. The way police gathered the information is even worse, because they simply copied license plate numbers without verifying that the registered owner was at the gathering.

This case wasn't unique. Other government bodies did even worse. The Illinois Public Aid Department began a matching program to uncover welfare cheats. However, because of deficient data, about half the "hits" it uncovered were false.

Official agencies are not the only ones with computer problems. Local retail credit bureaus are often sloppy in record-keeping, and merchants receive bad information. An example is that local bureaus don't pass information across state lines, and someone who has defaulted on debts can automatically get a clean record and a fresh start by moving to another state. Bankruptcy is another problem. If you declare bankruptcy, the credit bureau may have this information on file, but cannot disclose it because of a state privacy act.

TRW, a major national credit reporter, recently had a batch of bad data in its credit records for four New England states: Maine, New Hampshire, Rhode Island, and Vermont. Credit reports on individuals kept coming up with the same bad information — liens on property because of unpaid taxes. In Norwich, Vermont, a part-time employee of a subcontractor that supplies information to TRW mistakenly copied the names of all residents who had paid their taxes, instead of those who were delinquent. Similar incidents tainted data from other towns in the four states.[12]

Mailing list compilers also have their problems. In principle, they try to narrow the focus by targeting increasingly limited audiences. For example, a Republican political candidate might send an appeal for campaign funds to all members of the National Rifle Association living in his district. For obvious reasons, these would make better prospects than a list of welfare mothers. A company seeking to sell more credit cards uses a process called "pre-screening," in which a list of names aimed at a certain market segment is matched with a credit bureau's list of good credit risks. In theory, this should produce excellent results.

In practice, direct mail marketers consider a response rate of 5% to be good. A few years ago, 2% was the accepted standard for a good response rate. The improvement came from computer compilation and matching, but the net result is still that 95% or more of direct mail solicitations go into the garbage unanswered.

One evident reason is what we can call the "noise" factor. We receive a flood of junk mail, and most people don't have the time to read, and seriously consider, each offer. Each piece of advertising mail is competing for your attention with many others. The situation is so bad that some advertisers have resorted to deception to grab our attention. Some advertising comes in buff envelopes designed to look like those used by the government for mailing checks. Others are window envelopes with a printed form designed to resemble a check inside. We also become annoyed by the incessant barrage of junk mail flooding our mailboxes, and this leads to our disregarding anything which comes to us this way.

Another mundane reason is that Americans move often. Formerly, people used to remain at the same address for decades, or even their entire lives. Today, this is rare, and Americans are becoming more mobile than ever. This has a direct effect on junk mailers. To save money, junk mailers use economy-grade mailings which, unlike first-class, do not provide forwarding to a new address. This is why many pieces of junk mail, such as catalogs, are marked "or Current Resident." Any mailing list begins to go stale the moment it's compiled, and becomes progressively more obsolete with age.

Telephone marketers are having an increasingly hard time of it. In the normal course of events, they have to cope with a proportion of people who are not home, and other numbers returning "busy" signals. When they do connect, they encounter some people who are eating dinner, or who resent being interrupted while watching TV, or who have just come from the bathroom to answer the phone. More people now use answering machines to screen their calls, and don't pick up when the caller is selling something.

Notes

1. *Privacy in America*, David F. Linowes, Chicago, IL, University of Illinois Press, 1989, p. 77.

2. *Arizona Republic*, December 15 and 17, 1991.

3. *Privacy in America*, pp. 92-93.

4. *Understanding U.S. Identity Documents*, John Q. Newman, Port Townsend, WA, Loompanics Unlimited, 1991, pp. 136-138.

5. *Wall Street Journal*, March 14, 1991. Article by Michael W. Miller.

6. *Law and Order*, November, 1991, p. 23.

7. *Dossier Society*, Kenneth C. Laudon, New York, Columbia University Press, 1986, p. 32.

8. *Ibid.*, p. 34.

9. *How to Get Anything on Anybody, Book II*, Lee Lapin, San Mateo, CA, ISECO, Inc., 1991, pp. 158-159.

10. "The Pros and Cons of Proximity," Article by Mark Timms, *Security Management*, November, 1990, pp. 11A-12A.

11. *Arizona Republic*, July 7, 1988.

12. *Wall Street Journal*, October 14, 1991, article by Michael W. Miller.

11

Protecting Yourself

The future of private and government control over your life is grim for you. Without stretching the imagination, it's easy to see that a national system of identification cards might come on the scene one day, just as in many European countries. In France, anyone registering at a hotel must present his I.D. card or passport, and police officers scrutinize these every day. In Switzerland, it's required to register every change of address with the police. These are measures in countries we consider democratic. In repressive regimes, control measures, such as internal passports and travel permits, are even more onerous.

It's not enough to sweep for electronic taps or prepare false I.D. It's also unnecessary. Once the government decides you're worth wiretapping, you're in for more trouble than you can handle. You cannot protect yourself against electronic eavesdropping without special precautions and some very expensive equipment. The point is never to get to that stage. Remain out of their eyes, and you will most likely avoid special attention.

Living in America during the last decade of the 20th century means that your name is inevitably in one or more computer files, somewhere. It begins with your birth certificate, continues with your Social Security number, and before you're even old enough to vote, there's a lot of information on file about you.

Another problem comes with applying for employment. You can't deny an employer some information about yourself, and if the information doesn't check out, he simply won't hire you. Employers are becoming more aggressive in trying to find out as much about you as they can. Years ago, the rise of the American labor movement helped curb privacy invasion by employers, but the scene today is far different. Labor unions are becoming weaker each year as employers devise new and creative ways of union-busting. Media-inspired hysteria over illegal drugs has resulted in large-scale acceptance of drug screening as a routine condition of employment. All of these techniques result in more information about you entering one or more computer systems.

You can't avoid some attention. With the increasing cross-matching and exchange of information by government and private agencies, getting in one computer database means that you'll soon be in several.

The Morality of Self-protection

Is it moral to deny a government agency or private party accurate information about yourself? Is it right to slant information about yourself to "fake good?" Is it right to tell outright lies to benefit yourself? Some feel that all dishonesty is immoral, and refuse to dissemble in any way, even if they lose by being honest. This is why we must take a hard look at the cutting edge of power, to understand the situation as it really is, and not as the government or major commercial interests would like us to believe it is.

Despite Constitutional safeguards, the government has tremendous power over you, power it takes for granted and often uses unfairly. You may not be old enough to vote or drink alcohol, but you're old enough to go to jail if convicted of a crime. In some states, you're old enough to suffer capital punishment several years before you may legally vote or drink.

Several levels of government don't ask your permission before putting their hands in your pockets to extract money for taxes. They don't ask if you want the "services" they provide, but simply tell you that you must pay for them, like it or not. This is a legally-sanctioned protection racket.

Corporations have built a multi-billion dollar advertising industry to fake good to the consumer. Advertisers specialize in finding new and attractive ways to persuade you to buy products and services you don't want or need. They specialize in creative deception, faking good in the mass media. However, corporations expect job applicants to be perfectly honest about themselves.

When you apply for employment, you're getting into a vastly unequal relationship. A good example of this inequality is the way employers fire you. There's usually no notice, and there may even be a security guard to collect your employee badge, keys, and to escort you off the premises. If you decide to quit, however, employers demand two weeks' notice.

You're the solitary employee, trying to obtain a fair deal from a powerful employer with far greater resources than you have. He has the power to deny you employment, secure in the knowledge that others like you will line up for the job. The employer may also misrepresent the job or conditions of employment to you, or withhold vital information that might cause you to reconsider applying. When you finally find out that there are hidden conditions, you've quit your previous job, and it's too late to go back.

The power relationship is such that you're coerced into taking a variety of tests the employer may prescribe, but he'll tell you only what he chooses about himself and his company. The employer demands an honest and dedicated employee, but feels under no similar obligation to you. This is why you have to protect yourself and your interests. Deception is the weapon of the weak, and when dealing with an employer, you're in a very weak position indeed.

Avoiding Close Scrutiny

The situation we face in the last part of the 20th Century is unique in human history. Never before has it been possible for both government and private interests to track masses of people as individuals. Even during eras when slavery was common, the most a slave-owner could do was to put a brand or mark upon his slaves' bodies to identify them. If a slave succeeded in running away, eluding the grasp of his or her former master, it was possible to make a new start in another land.

This was even possible, and common, in 19th Century America. Many left the East Coast for the frontier, because they knew that they could leave their pasts behind them and make new starts. Today, the frontier is closed. In fact, the entire society is closed. Those who tried to "drop out" during the 1960s found this out very clearly.

Today, it's simply not possible to keep to yourself outside government scrutiny and control. The means of surveillance and control are so varied and widespread that it's impossible to avoid them all. Even if you were born in a wood shack out in the hills, thereby avoiding official registration via a birth certificate, you would not be able to keep out of the clutches of government. Entering school would put you into an official record. You'd be required to have a medical examination and present certificates of vaccination. Getting a job would put you into the Internal

Revenue Service's computers. Even obtaining an apartment, drivers license, or buying property would place your name into a variety of private and official records.

No matter how determined you may be to drop out, society won't let you. Every piece of land in this country is either privately owned or under government control. Even if you decided to become a "mountain man," like Claude Dallas, the government would not leave you in peace. Game and fish officers would track you down, and unless you lived exclusively on bark and berries, would cite you for hunting without a license or out of season. They might even cite you for trespassing in certain areas, because of regulations regarding where you might set up camp. Park police and game officers enforce these regulations with the full power of the law behind them.

Changing your identity is another way to discard a past. However, it puts you under some strict limitations. Where do you obtain your new identity? Do you create a name and background off the top of your head? If so, remember that your new cover will be very superficial, and won't stand up to any investigation.

You can forge a drivers license, but if a police officer stops you for a routine traffic offense, he'll collect your license and vehicle registration. He'll check you out for outstanding warrants, just in case you're a wanted fugitive. This is the negative check. He'll also verify your license and registration by radio with the motor vehicle bureau. If there's no record of you, you'll be in for an intense investigation.

This also precludes your obtaining employment with any government agency, and with many large corporations. You'll be limited to working in low-level occupations, where employers don't bother with employee screening, such as dishwasher, fruit picker, etc. If you seek employment with a large company, you'll have to survive pre-employment screening.

Pre-employment screening is complex, and covers much more ground than in the past. Previously a check of the most recent references and a criminal history check were enough. Today, it's very different, because of the doctrine of "positive vetting," or verification. This arose from the need to thoroughly check out employment applicants, especially those for sensitive positions.

The reason for positive vetting was that foreign agents either came equipped with fabricated documents or adopted another person's identity, and a casual check was insufficient to uncover this. In Pre-World War II Britain, for example, a security clearance was merely a check with the files of Scotland Yard and the Security Service, DI-5. If no negative information turned up, the request was returned marked "N.T." (No Trace), or "N. L. T." (No Likely Trace), if the file clerk didn't feel like running a total search. This was sloppy work, and permitted many unreliable people to obtain sensitive positions.

When security officers realized that this led to massive leaks, they turned to positive verification. This means that, instead of merely checking for negative factors such as a criminal history, investigators seek to verify positively everything about your background, such as place and date of birth, school records, previous addresses, etc. They'll inspect your school records, speak with former neighbors and landlords, and spend many hours simply confirming that you were at a certain place when you said you were. If you don't have a documented past, you simply won't get the job, and you might even face inquiries about your elusive history.

The trick is to have a plain-vanilla documented past. Of course you went to school, like everyone else. Of course you bought a car, and received a traffic ticket or two, like most others. You also had the usual childhood diseases, and perhaps had your tonsils out. You want to blend in with the crowd, to avoid curiosity and further investigation.

An Example

At this point, let's see how this information-gathering power can serve sinister purposes. We'll select a hypothetical extremist group, the ABCs, to see how they would gather data on the XYZs, a religious denomination they want to track for future action. Let's further assume that the ABCs use only legal means, and that under no circumstances will they burglarize premises or take any other action which would violate the law.

A first step would be to compile a list of anyone who is or might be an XYZ, using publicly-available information. Scanning telephone directories for names and addresses can provide many that either are obviously XYZish or sound XYZish. Checking city directories, such as *Polk's* or *Cole's*, ABC members can find names and address not listed in the official phone books. These go into a database for further processing.

Knowing that many XYZs changed their names to blend in with mainstream people, the ABC group takes further steps to uncover them. One way is to hire a news clipping service to save all articles on the particular religion and its organizations. Fund-raisers, annual balls, holidays, and other social events often rate a few lines or a photograph in the local paper. There may be an article that "John Smith" has just been elected President of the congregation at an XYZ religious institution, and this pinpoints Smith and his relatives as being XYZs. There may also be articles about the "XYZ Anti-Defamation League," which further identifies members.

Birth and death announcements often contain information relating to the subject's religion. Obituaries often list names of survivors. Wedding announcements also provide this information, and often provide guests' names. Scout troops sponsored by religious organizations also provide solid leads to the affiliations of members and their families. Newspaper articles dealing with the activities of troops affiliated with the XYZ organization or church always provide a few names, and sometimes photos.

As the database expands, it serves to uncover further links. Once the ABC group knows, for example, that "John Smith" is an XYZ, they can have their clipping service save any newspaper articles about him. If he's a public figure, there will be some articles, but even if he's not, wedding, birth, and death announcements including his name can provide leads.

Another way is to set up an observation post near a congregation. This can be a rented room, the home of a member who actually lives nearby, or a parked camper. ABC members conducting surveillance will record license plate numbers of cars parked during services. Most states will divulge names and addresses of vehicle registrations, upon demand, for a small fee.

An ABC member can join an XYZ group, pretending to be one of them. He doesn't have to do anything daring or spectacular to obtain information, because James Bond stunts are both out of place and unnecessary. It's enough to attend meetings, pay dues, and meet people. Members usually receive membership lists, and with a little work the undercover ABC member can obtain photographs of many of the congregation. By simply listening, he can obtain information about XYZ people who are not affiliated with that particular congregation.

In any organization, there's a need for volunteers to address envelopes and do other mundane work. This makes it unnecessary to steal mailing lists or other documents, or to burglarize the clergyman's office to obtain names of people for whom he's performed religious ceremonies. Simply putting in a few hours each month to help address the organization's newsletter, then volunteering to drop the envelopes off at the post office on the way home, can provide access to the list.

ABC members in special positions can obtain information not publicly available, but at no risk. Anyone working in a hospital can often find out the religious affiliation of a patient, because this is often on a patient's chart. A postal mail carrier can look for religious symbols on doors during his normal workday. An undertaker can scan the guest book at every funeral of a member of the XYZ faith, certain to find co-religionists as well as friends.

ABC members can also conduct pro-active operations to uncover "closet" XYZs. One way is to place classified ads in singles' magazines for a new "XYZ Singles Group," using a mail drop as a return address. As long as they don't solicit money, there's no fraud charge possible. When responses come in, they provide more leads for uncovering XYZish people trying to maintain low profiles, as well as the overt ones.

Thus we see that gathering information about people is both legal and easy, using only easily-available sources. The use to which a group puts the information may be extremely illegal, but banning information-gathering is even more futile than passing gun control laws.

Enter The Phantom

For special activities, you need a layer of protection which we'll call simply the "phantom." This is a false and totally non-existent person, who never obtains any official paperwork, but who serves as a stand-in for you when you want to do something controversial. It's not illegal to use another name, as long as it's not for fraudulent purposes. The phantom cannot protect you against a serious official investigation of criminal charges, but will defeat practically any casual or private investigation.

You can't have the phantom apply for a job, because positive verification would show that no such person exists. You also can't obtain a drivers license for him, because this would be illegal. What you can do, though, is obtain cashier's checks and money orders in his name, and list his address as "care of" yourself. We'll study other ways of creating a phantom identity as we examine various privacy-protection tactics.

Protection Against Police Surveillances

Police agents may wiretap you, or obtain a search warrant for a physical inspection. There's no absolute protection against these methods, but you can avoid stacking the odds in their favor.

First, assume all telephone conversations are being monitored, especially if you have a mobile, portable, or cellular phone. Don't say anything on the telephone that you don't want to see on the front page of the *New York Times* tomorrow. Also avoid sensitive conversations in unfamiliar premises, especially a security office or a police station. You can be sure these are bugged.

If you have to discuss something very confidential with someone, pick a remote location, and when you arrive, take him or her somewhere else. That makes it very hard for eavesdroppers to plant microphones on you.

If you suspect someone of "wearing a wire," a tape recorder, one countermeasure is to physically search him, paying special attention to the small of the back and the crotch. If this isn't practical, say as little as possible. Answer with nods and shrugs instead of saying "yes" or "no."[1]

Don't carry sensitive materials in a car if possible. Remember that laws and court decisions on what parts of a car are open to search without a warrant keep changing.

At your home or office, keep the door locked, and don't admit anyone you don't know. If a police officer shows up with a warrant, read it before admitting him.

These precautions work mainly when dealing with official police. Private investigators are more likely to use subterfuge and surreptitious searches than official police. Private security officers have less authority, but are more free-wheeling, which is why their reputation is much worse than the cops.

Financial Privacy

You might think that, if it's impossible to drop out totally, you can at least keep your name out of as many data banks as possible by living without credit cards or checking accounts, leaving as small a paper trail as possible. This is the philosophy of privacy advocates, but isn't practical for several reasons. Actually, this is very hard to do, and by itself can attract attention. If you deal only in cash, for example, you can get by in making small purchases. However, trying to pay for a car with a suitcase full of bills would attract a lot of attention because it's so unusual. In fact, keeping large amounts of cash today screams "drug trafficker" to government investigators.

A 1984 federal law requires businesses to report any cash payment exceeding $10,000 to the IRS. This is aimed at people trying to launder money and at other racketeers. Stricter IRS enforcement now requires businesses to report any transaction involving liquid cash substitutes, such as cashier's checks. This is similar to the law requiring banks to report cash deposits or withdrawals of $10,000 or more, or amounts apparently designed to circumvent the limit, such as a withdrawal of $9,999.[2]

Maintaining total financial privacy is impossible. If you have any income, it's subject to scrutiny because all or part might be taxable. Almost anything you buy generates a record, and how extensive this record is depends partly on your mode of payment.

Paying cash, of course, leaves no trace, and it's perfectly practical for most items you buy over-the-counter, such as liquor, condoms, sex toys, or pornography. Although many "adult" stores and telephone-fantasy concerns accept credit cards, if you pay this way you'll create a paper trail and a permanent record of your transaction.

For mail-order purchases, money orders, traveler's checks, and cashier's checks are anonymous, because you can pay for them with cash at point of purchase, and don't have to show I.D.

The IRS requires you to make a financial statement each year: Form 1040 in one of its various forms. Logically, you declare only what the IRS can trace. If you're earning cash on the side, the IRS can't identify it unless your lifestyle is so lavish that it's out of proportion to your declared income.

One aspect of financial privacy you can keep under your control is your personal financial records. You can keep them in a private vault, so that even a search warrant served upon your home or business won't reveal them. This may become necessary because records in the hands of your attorney, accountant, bank, or employees are open to seizure by search warrant.

Securing your personal records requires that nobody but yourself know about them. A search warrant can open any door, but no government or police agency, or grand jury, can issue a search warrant for something it doesn't know exists, or at least doesn't know where it might be. Safe deposit boxes are secure only up to the point where they can be seized by the government. This is why private vaults have sprung up around the country in recent years. Safeguarding your private business from prying eyes can require establishing another address, and the only ways to do this without forging I.D. documents or otherwise breaking the law are to hire a secretarial service or to rent an office or apartment away from home.

Control of Information

The best way to retain control of information about yourself is not to let it get out in the first place. The slogan, "Three can keep a secret if two of them are dead," attributed to a biker gang, sounds very macho and businesslike, but it's also misleading. Instead of bumping off people to whom you've passed sensitive information, it's easier not to tell them in the first place.

Never provide any information about yourself unless you absolutely have to. Applying for employment is one of these no-win propositions, but don't give anything away in other situations. One example is compilers of city directories, who go door to door requesting information in the manner of census-takers. There is, however, a right way and a wrong way to turn them away. If you adopt a hostile attitude and absolutely refuse to answer any questions, you'll attract attention. It's better to find a way to avoid answering questions. A simple answer to anyone who asks for information about the residents is to say that you're merely housesitting for the occupants, who are away in Europe. You can give them a false name, or give totally imaginary information about the "occupants." You may also plead ignorance, saying that you simply answered an ad, and know almost nothing about the occupants. Obviously, never give any personal information over the phone, either, no matter who the caller pretends to be.

Refusing to give information over the phone also helps you to avoid one of the latest scams practiced by con artists. Some-one pretending to be a representative of a long-distance company telephones you to say that you've been charged with long-distance calls several hours long. The fake representative asks for your telephone credit card number to make sure it doesn't happen again. If you hesitate, the representative may threaten to disconnect your service for lack of cooperation. Actually, your long-distance carrier already knows your card number, and no legitimate representative needs to ask for it over the phone. If you provide your number, members of these rings flash it to confederates all over the country, and soon you're being billed for calls made from other states.[3]

One of the worst situations to encounter is the intrusive employer who is not only interested in how well you can do the job, but who wants to get into your mind as well. In one sense, you're more vulnerable than if you were dealing with the government, because there are truly few effective legal protections against an intrusive employer.

Don't be afraid to lie to protect your interests. Employers are very afraid of applicants who lie to them, and have taken many steps to prevent or discourage falsification. One simple step is the threat, printed on the employment application, that any falsification will be cause for dismissal. Another is the statement that responses will be checked. A study showed that applicants informed that their statements would be checked lied less.[4] Thus, because this study originated over 16 years ago, the word has gotten around among employers that applicants can be bluffed in this, as well. Don't be afraid to lie! Let them catch you if they can.

The key to presenting effective lies is common sense. Don't claim a tremendous background that you don't have, or try to deny any and all faults. Nobody's perfect, and trying to pass yourself off as a perfect person will kick back at you because it's just not credible. Instead, lie with a light touch. Let's look at specific applications.

When you're forced to disclose information about yourself, follow a few simple rules. When filling out an employment application, taking a psychological test, or applying for a loan, try to appear as average and unexciting as possible. "Fake good," but not beyond the limit of credibility.

For example, you can admit to having failed a course in college, or having received traffic citations. You may also admit to having taken some stationery from a previous employer, or used his telephone for personal calls. In short, admit the minor faults common to most people. Do not fall victim to the "salami-slicing" technique, in which the interviewer obtains a minor damaging admission from you, then pushes you to admit more serious ones.

Do not let an interviewer's kind and sympathetic attitude fool you into thinking you can trust him. They're experts in adopting a "non-judgmental" manner to fool people into relaxing their defenses.

NEVER, NEVER, NEVER admit to anything serious, no matter how sympathetic or intimidating an interviewer might be, or how much you want a job or insurance policy. If you were once arrested for auto theft, let them find it out themselves. Don't lay it out on a platter for them. If you were treated for alcoholism or drug dependency, do not admit it, especially if you're asked to list it on a form and sign your name. If you were fired from a previous job for theft, likewise. The odds are that, unless you were arrested and convicted, this will never come to light.

There are two reasons for this. One is important. The other is crucial. First, admitting to any felony is likely to preclude your being hired. The door will slam shut in your face, leaving you wondering what happened. More importantly, the information goes into your record, somewhere. Instead of losing the opportunity for one job, you now compromise your entire future. Your application or test results may surface again, when a future employer runs a computer check on you, and will haunt you for the rest of your life.

If you claim employment with a company now out of business to fill a gap in your job history, remember to make it con-

sistent with what can be checked. Investigators keep old telephone books and business directories on hand, and if you claim
employment during a period when the defunct company had
already ceased to exist, your statement is open to question.

Another ploy that arouses suspicion among mean-minded in-
terviewers is claiming to have been a "consultant," or "self-em-
ployed."[5] The interviewer may well ask you for the names of
a couple of your "customers." Remember to backstop yourself
by arranging for a couple of friends to provide favorable
references.

The same principle of plausibility holds when taking "personality tests" or "attitude surveys." You'll encounter questions such
as:

"I sometimes get impatient with people."

"My mood often swings up and down."

"Sometimes, I think of killing myself."

"I don't like everyone I meet."

"I sometimes get strange ideas."

"I get unhappy sometimes."

"I once took something that didn't belong to me."

"People are out to get me."

"My work sometimes bores me."

"People talk about me behind my back."

"I feel nervous when taking tests."

When answering such questions, try to appear credible. It's
all right if your work sometimes bores you, or that you may get
impatient with people at times. You may even have taken
something that was not yours, or be occasionally unhappy. It's

a red flag if you admit to thinking of suicide, having strange ideas, or other bizarre thoughts. If you state that people are out to get you, or talk about you behind your back, you're in real trouble.

Above all, remember that, although an employer can check the truth of your school or employment record by running a background check on you, there is no way he can find out what's really inside your head unless you tell him. Anyone who claims otherwise is simply a test salesman promoting his self-interest.

You may encounter word-matching or free-association tests. There are also ink-blot tests, in which the tester will ask you what an inkblot resembles. The key to getting by on these is avoiding bizarre or violent responses. If an inkblot looks like a dead body, don't admit it. If the word "shell" makes you think of "shell-fire," substitute "sea shell." Avoid any blood-and-guts answers, and any that display aggression or hostility.

Some types of "attitude surveys" are politically loaded, designed to detect attitudes employers don't like. There are questions such as these:

"Do you feel that breaking the law is sometimes justified?"

"Does society have too many rules to follow?"

"Do employees steal because their bosses don't treat them well?"

"Are big businessmen bigger crooks than employees?"

Generally, you should answer "no" to this type of question, but even that may not get you off the hook because some testers use very convoluted reasoning. Some feel that people are very cynical today, and would answer "yes" to many such questions. Only the crook, according to this logic, would answer "no."

Unless you're applying for police or security jobs, you're unlikely to have to submit to a polygraph test as a condition of employment. If you do, don't let it intimidate you. Although, as we've seen, the polygraph is unreliable, its proponents still advocate its use because many subjects confess. According to J. Kirk Barefoot, speaking for the American Polygraph Association, some make damaging admissions even before the start of the test.[6]

This is why, if you have to take a polygraph examination, you must be prepared. Study what the polygraph can and cannot do, and how polygraph operators intimidate their subjects. Once you take the test, never admit that any answer was untrue, no matter how the operator may try to badger you by suggesting that a certain answer has produced a "problem."

Controlling Other Information

Control of information about sensitive topics is crucial in all contexts, and a lot of this is totally within your control. Let's look at a few examples.

If you have a safe deposit box, do not deduct it on your tax return. The IRS allows the deduction, which is a concession that provides the IRS a lead to a strongbox that might contain hidden or undeclared assets. You may prefer to maintain a bank safe deposit box, instead of relying on a private vault service, if private vaults charge much more than banks in your area for comparably-sized boxes. Another reason might be that there are no privately-operated vaults in your area. If you have enough money on deposit to rate a premium service from your bank, take advantage of it. Some services include free checking and a free safe deposit box. This can be important, because with a free box, you won't be billed for its use, and your bank statement won't contain deductions for the box — a very important point if you're trying to keep something hidden.

Another class of allowable deductions is political contributions. If you support an unpopular political group, or one which you feel may be outlawed soon, be careful. Although in theory we are free to hold whatever political beliefs we wish, in practice this isn't so. Do not link yourself to it on your tax return by deducting your contribution. Forego the temptation to squeeze every last deduction from your income tax form, and keep your secret to yourself.

If you need to see a psychiatrist, don't charge it to your medical insurance. This might be an expense you don't want to pay, but paying it from your pocket is better than having it in your medical insurance records, from which the information might end up many other places. If you want to be really secure, use the "phantom."

The same is true if you want to have an HIV test. Your girlfriend might insist that you get tested because she's worried about AIDS. However, some of your friends and co-workers, and most investigators, will assume that you're getting tested because you're bisexual or homosexual. If you want an HIV test, go to another doctor, use a phantom name, and pay for it out of your pocket. The mere notation in your medical history that you asked for an HIV test, even if the result was negative, could have severe repercussions for you because of the AIDS hysteria. Keep in mind that company-sponsored medical insurance often results in the paperwork being processed where you work. The information that you had an HIV test would make a juicy bit of workplace gossip.

Some medical care is best obtained out of state. Abortions, for example, are controversial, and if you want to have one, keep it a secret. Go to another state, or even another country, to avoid the stigma. Likewise for sex-change surgery. It's unlikely to become generally accepted in the near future, and it attracts unpleasant labels.

Be careful regarding what you tell a doctor, especially a psychiatrist. Some will not consider it a violation of medical ethics to reveal certain information, such as suicidal thoughts, child molesting, etc. Be aware that, in some states, anyone with knowledge of child abuse is bound to notify the authorities. This includes doctors, teachers, counselors, and others. If you are seeking professional help because of a tendency to molest children, you'll be putting your head in the noose.

Results can be bizarre in some situations. Hypothetically, let's assume you're seeking help because you find yourself sexually attracted to your children, and your shrink decides to inform on you because he feels that the danger to your children, although you haven't actually done anything, is more important than your privacy. Child protection agencies have sweeping powers, and you could find child protection agents taking custody of your children without what we consider due process. You'd face a long and hard court fight to get them back, especially because you'd have to struggle against information provided by your psychiatrist, who'd be using your own words against you without a Miranda warning. In short, you'd be guilty until proven innocent.

Some people buy trouble because they cannot keep their mouths shut. One example is an interview with the press. Public figures can't avoid the media, because their careers thrive on publicity. If you're not a public figure, you have a legally enforceable right to privacy, but the first step in maintaining that right is to avoid blabbing to the press. Reporters supposedly "respect" confidentiality, but don't bet on it. It's far safer to assume that anything you say to a reporter will be on Page One tomorrow. That way, you'll avoid nasty surprises.

Another problem is that police agencies may subpoena reporters' notes, or require them to testify before a grand jury. While some reporters will go to jail before breaking a confidence, others will talk. Police officers with search warrants can enter a newspaper office, just as they can enter a doctor's or lawyer's office. Therefore, if you really want to keep something quiet, don't tell the press.

Yet another problem is distortion or misquoting. There have been enough cases of reporters taking statements out of context to make some people, such as police officers, very careful regarding what they say to a reporter. Some reporters use tape recorders to ensure the accuracy of their quotes, but others do not. One case, in which a reporter fabricated quotes she attributed to the person she interviewed, is still in litigation.

Therefore, unless there's a compelling reason to seek personal publicity, stonewall all media questions. Simply answering "I don't know anything" to all questions will frustrate and discourage a reporter.

Consent Forms

When applying for employment or insurance, you may encounter a request to sign a consent form allowing the release of medical or other personal information to your employer or insurer. You're in a bad spot, because although he can't force you to sign, he doesn't have to grant you a job or an insurance policy, either. This places you in a very weak position. The best you can do is refuse to sign a blanket authorization. Don't sign a short form that requests release of any and all information without specifying limits. The release should be good only for a limited period, and to specific sources.

Third-party Investigations

Your name can turn up during an investigation totally unrelated to you. If DEA agents decide that your family doctor has been dispensing more than the "normal" amount of prescription narcotics or mood-altering drugs, they may obtain a search warrant and scrutinize his medical records, examining each patient's file in the search for a pattern of violations.

Dr. Gary Hall, an eye surgeon in Phoenix, Arizona, found his home invaded by FBI agents one day in December, 1991. He was not charged with any crime, nor necessarily under suspicion. The reason for the search was that he is the son-in-law of Charles Keating, under federal indictment for racketeering in the Lincoln Savings and Loan collapse. A federal judge had issued a court order freezing Keating's assets and personal property to prevent Keating from "attempting to transfer property subject to forfeiture." FBI agents collected an inventory of all of Keating's property, including personal property, and all of his relatives' property, including Dr. Hall.[7]

Some tax preparers and accountants skirt the edge of the law, and even help clients hide assets and "pad" deductions to obtain lower tax liabilities. If discovered, not only does the IRS prosecute them, but it closely examines the tax returns of their entire client lists in the hope of uncovering more frauds. If your tax preparer has several clients who have submitted questionable returns, the IRS will scrutinize all of his clients, including you, looking for frauds and evasions.

High Times, a monthly magazine devoted to marijuana use and legalization, was the target of federal investigators. Subpoenas sought to obtain the names, addresses, and telephone numbers of all employees and former employees.[8]

The Ultimate Information Control

Setting up a new identity is the ultimate way to shed a past, and present a smiling new face to the future. This, however, is easier said than done, because government bureaucrats also read the "how-to" books, and have devised certain countermeasures.

As we've seen, the "phantom" is a rudimentary form of new identity, but this method won't take you very far. Your phantom won't be able to apply for a driver's license, or passport, and this restricts him to a narrow range of usefulness.

One axiom that almost nobody mentions is that, if you think you might need a new I.D. in the future, the time to begin setting it up is now. Any identity you set up must "age" to increase its effectiveness.[9] Not only must you have documents that appear to be as old as their dates, but it helps if you've had business dealings, such as a bank account, under your new identity. Any independent verification that your alter ego has been active for a certain amount of time enhances his credibility.

How To Find Out What They Know About You

It's sometimes possible to find out the information in your file, but this has its limits. You can, theoretically, find out if the FBI has a file on you, under the Freedom of Information Act, but this isn't very helpful. The FBI will release only routine and meaningless information. They won't tell you if there's a current investigation on you. They'll also black out the names of any informers who have put the mouth on you.

Your insurance company may provide you with a "privacy statement" as discussed earlier. State and federal laws often require that a company provide a reason if they turn you down. In practice, this is hard to obtain without persistence. The first tactic is to "stonewall" you, depending upon your ignorance. You may get a letter stating that release of this information is prohibited because of your state's "privacy act." Enough people fall for this nonsense to make it a useful tactic. If you receive such a reply, write or phone back asking the title and number of the law they're citing. This often deflates their argument. Another way is to contact your state's department of insurance. One of their personnel will be able to tell you if there is indeed a privacy act prohibiting giving a person his own records.

Credit bureaus are regulated by federal law, and must provide you with a copy of your records. But getting it isn't as easy as it seems.

First, many ask that you complete a form in which you provide them with even more information than they already have. Another problem is that many of these forms are in code, mainly designed for brevity, but which makes them incomprehensible to the outsider. TRW actually has turned this confusion into extra revenue by selling a service to interpret your own credit report. A third problem is that some of their information depends on input from other agencies, which you then must contact to obtain a complete picture of what's on file on you. Finally, some companies, such as TRW, charge fees for disclosure.[10]

Addresses of the major credit bureaus are:

Equifax
P.O. Box 4081
Atlanta, GA 30302   Phone: 404-885-8000

Trans Union has three addresses, one for each region:
Trans Union East
P.O. Box 360
Philadelphia, PA 19105   Phone: 215-569-4582

Trans Union Midwest Consumer Relations
222 S. First Street, Suite 201
Louisville, KY 40202   Phone: 502-584-0121

Trans Union West
P.O. Box 3110
Fullerton, CA 92634   Phone: 714-738-3800

TRW Credit Data
National Consumer Relations Center
12606 Greenville Avenue
P.O. Box 749029
Dallas, TX 75374-9029   Phone: 214-235-1200
                                    Extension 251

The Medical Information Bureau's address is:
Medical Information Bureau
P.O. Box 105, Essex Station
Boston, MA 02112   Phone: (617) 426-3660

Mail-order Investigations

One way of tracing what happens to your name when you fill out a form is to code it with a middle initial. Unless it's an official form, such as a passport application, you can do this without any kickback. When filling out a warranty registration, for example, write your name as "John A. Smith" for one, and "John B. Smith" for the next. If you keep a list, you'll be able to see what each company did with your name and address.

Be careful of joining organizations. Although as Americans we're supposed to have a degree of political freedom many of the world's citizens don't, many Americans have found out otherwise. During the 1930s, for example, some joined a variety of left-wing organizations that ten years later were on a government list of "subversive" or "Communist front" organizations. This barred them from sensitive jobs, and caused some of them to be summoned before investigating committees.

Buy controversial publications over the counter. Never subscribe to them because subscription lists of publications such as *High Times* are scanned by DEA agents.

Don't put return addresses on your envelopes when sending anything controversial, such as a contribution to an off-beat political party. If the address is clear, there's no reason for a return address.

Don't put your full name and address at the bottom of a letter, either, unless it's a "plain vanilla" communication that is in no way compromising to you. Legally or not, postal inspectors and other investigators can open mail without your becoming aware of it.

Be careful what you buy through the mail under your own name. If you're into kinky sex, or even normal sex toys such as ribbed condoms, your name will go on a mailing list if you buy them by mail. These companies sell their mailing lists, as do other concerns.

If you want to order material that may be controversial, but is definitely not illegal, such as pornography and sex toys, you can do it under a false name using the "phantom" technique. Simply buy a money order under an alias, say "John Smith," and have the material delivered to John Smith care of yourself, at your address. You can then get rid of any marketers following up on this person and address by saying that "John Smith" doesn't live there any more, and has left no forwarding address. This works beautifully for anything that is not criminal.

Another defense is to prepare a false address for special purposes. If you absolutely must have something incriminating shipped to you, arrange for it to be shipped to your secret address, and this doesn't mean a P.O. box or a mail drop, unless you've been able to obtain one under another identity.

Renting a mail drop under another name isn't as hard as it may seem. You must be prepared to show I.D., but a forged or altered drivers license is perfectly adequate, as the mail drop operator won't scrutinize it as closely as a police officer would. A Polaroid copy with suitably altered name and address will do, as long as you keep it inside the plastic envelope in your wallet.

One way of obtaining a legitimate P.O. box without leaving your identity is if you have a friend with a box who is leaving the area. He may be willing to hand over his key, if you continue to make the payments.

It's possible to rent a mail drop box for a phantom, to avoid linking certain types of mail to your name. The trick is to rent it for a "business," which allows you to list several corporate officers by name as recipients of individually addressed mail. For example, you rent a mail drop under your real name, calling it "John Smith Enterprises." On the form, you list phantom names such as "Jack Jones" and "Jim Brown" as partners, who also will receive mail through the drop. This lets you use these phantoms to receive pornography, controversial books, and other materials that would put their names on lists you wish to avoid.

If a mail drop is your choice, follow a couple of fine points to keep in character and avoid arousing suspicion. If you rent it under an assumed name, you won't want to pay the fee with a check or bank card in your real name. You may start an account under your phantom name, or you may pay in cash. If you're renting a box as a firm, remember to ask for receipts, because real businesses deduct rental fees on their tax returns.

Yet another way is to hire a secretarial service and arrange for them to take your mail. This can be expensive, but in certain situations, worth the money.

Another plan is filing a change-of-address card for a totally unrelated address, and then using that as a mailing address. The phantom's mail then would get forwarded to your address. The main drawback is that it's risky because the postal carrier on that route may realize that nobody by that name had received mail there before the change of address card came through.

You could also rent an apartment or office solely for the purpose of obtaining a mailing address. This can be very expensive, but it's practically fool-proof. You don't need to fill out any official paperwork, and in most cases landlords don't run an extensive check on prospective tenants. Many simply go by first impression and gut-level logic. If you look respectable, wear your hair short, and don't wear fancy jewelry or heavy perfume, you'll pass inspection.

Firearms

Every firearm you buy today from a dealer leaves a paper trail. In most cases, this is innocuous, because the only record remains with the dealer, unless you live in a jurisdiction that has gun registration or licensing laws. Bureau of Alcohol, Tobacco, and Firearms agents do not routinely ask dealers to turn over their records, partly because they don't have the personnel to process them. A little-known provision of the federal gun control law requires a dealer to file Form 3310.4 when the same person buys more than one handgun within five consecutive business days. The dealer must get this form in the mail the same day. This sets up a red flag in the local ATF office, and your name will routinely be run through the computer for a criminal records check. You may also be checked out against lists of subversive organizations, and other lists, to assess your potential as a threat to law and order. The BATF "considers multiple sales reports to be an excellent investigative tool."[11]

Buying firearms from private parties should be a cash deal, for several reasons. The first is to avoid leaving a paper trail, as a check does. Another is that cash passes without question, while some people feel uncomfortable taking a check from a stranger. It's futile, however, to pay cash for a firearm bought from a dealer, because of the federal registration form.

Striking Back

There are ways to strike back at those collecting information about you. The simplest way is to be totally uncooperative. This works only in certain situations, such as when you receive a questionnaire in the mail. If you refuse to fill out an employment application, you won't get the job.

Marketing Services

Sabotaging commercial information gathering programs is very easy. Whenever you get the opportunity, give them false information, even creating non-existent persons. This is more effective than just throwing away the forms, because the company distributing the forms pays someone to enter this information into its computer, and can end up spending a lot of money following a false lead before it discovers that the return is fictitious.

Another way is to take advantage of any offer of free items to those who apply for credit cards, shopping cards, etc., by filling out several forms with false names and addresses. Some supermarket chains doing this hand each person a coupon for free food in return for each completed questionnaire. They then go to the expense of producing a credit card and mailing it to each person listed. The only limitation is that, when the Post Office returns the envelopes as undeliverable, they'll wipe the records from their computer. The way around this is to be prepared with real names and addresses, taken from the telephone directory.

Junk Mail

If you really resent junk mail, make it a point never to buy anything by mail-order or to reply to any mail advertisements. Companies sell their lists, and even replying to a contest offer without buying anything gets you on a list because you read and responded to the mailing.

When you receive junk mail, don't just throw it away. Open every envelope, and if a business reply card or envelope is enclosed, drop it in the mail, blank. The company will have to pay the postage, even for a blank card or empty envelope.

If you have a little time to spare, fill out the cards with fictitious names and addresses to clutter their files and make them waste postage. Eventually, they'll purge their files, but meanwhile they'll spend resources and postage mailing to non-existent people.

Intrusive Employers

If you neither smoke nor use illegal drugs, you can strike back against employers who ban smoking and require job applicants to take urine tests. Apply for a job you don't want. After you pass the urine test and return for an interview, carry an open pack of cigarettes in your pocket, and ask why there is a smoking ban. Whatever the answer, pull out your cigarette pack and state that if you smoke or use drugs off-duty, that's your business alone. This will make the employer doubt the effectiveness of the urine test.

Notes

1. *Low Profile*, William Petrocelli, New York, McGraw-Hill, 1981, p. 209.
2. Associated Press, November 25, 1991.
3. *Arizona Republic*, September 5, 1991.
4. W. F. Cascio, "Accuracy of Verifiable Biographical Information Blank Responses," *Journal of Applied Psychology*, Vol. 60, No. 6, 1975, pp. 767-769.
5. "Checking the Personals," article by William A. Sharp, *Security Management*, April 1991, p. 39.
6. *Low Profile*, p. 102.
7. *Arizona Republic*, December 15, 1991.

8. *The Drug Policy Letter*, May/June 1991, p. 9.
9. *Understanding U.S. Identity Documents*, John Q. Newman, Port Townsend, WA, Loompanics Unlimited, 1991, pp. 139-143.
10. *Wall Street Journal*, September 23, 1991. Article by Michael W. Miller.
11. *FFL Newsletter*, 1991 Volume 1, p. 4.

12

Summing Up

This examination of the latest trends in Big Brotherism has turned up some frightening facts. Foremost is the vastly increased information processing power available even to small private parties keeping databases. The government is limited by various privacy laws, and its operations are, theoretically at least, subject to public scrutiny and control. Private operations are mostly uncontrolled, and those kept out of sight are beyond the reach of any investigation or law.

The bright part is that, in most cases, database operators only know what you choose to tell them. Information processing is not the same as information gathering, which still requires a lot of leg-work and knocking on doors. If you have the understanding and maturity to practice discretion, and if you don't allow yourself to be bulldozed, you can still avoid Big Brother.

13

For Further Reading

Applicant Investigation Techniques in Law Enforcement, John P. Harlan, Ed.D., and Patrick A. Mueller, J.D., Springfield, IL, Charles C. Thomas, Publisher, 1985. This is a nuts-and-bolts book outlining techniques and resources.

Brotherhood of Murder, Thomas Martinez and John Gunther, NY, Pocket Books, 1988. A good true-crime book with valuable information on police information-gathering.

Confessions of an Ex-Secret Service Agent, George Rush, NY, Pocket Star Books, 1991. This book provides an insider's view of what it's like to be a Secret Service agent. It's not always flattering to the Secret Service, because it lays out clearly some of the nonsense and regimentation the Service imposes upon its officers.

Confidential Information Sources, Public and Private, Second Edition, John M. Carroll, Boston, Butterworth-Heinemann, 1991. This is a bible of information gathering, the most comprehensive description of tools and techniques contained in one volume.

Deception Detection, Charles Clifton, Boulder, CO, Paladin Press, 1991. This 145-page volume is the best written on the subject, and tells you what you need to know to defend yourself against a polygraph operator. Remember, you're not fighting the "box," which is just a box full of wires and electronic components. You're up against a human operator, who will even lie to produce a confession.

Deep Cover, Police Intelligence Operations, Burt Rapp, Boulder, CO, Paladin Press, 1989. This is a practical, no-nonsense book about police intelligence operations, concentrating on how they gather information on people, manage the information, and how they disseminate it.

Dossier: The Secret Files They Keep on You, Aryeh Neier, NY, Stein and Day, 1975. This is a slightly paranoid view of the files THEY are keeping on YOU. Written by an official of the ACLU, this does paint a grim picture, but one grimmer than justified by the situation.

Dossier Society, Kenneth C. Laudon, NY, Columbia University Press, 1986. This book follows the lines of *Dossier,* but is more up-to-date.

The Drug Policy Letter, May/June 1991. This newsletter provides the latest news on illegal drugs and government policies.

How to Get Anything on Anybody, Lee Lapin, San Francisco, Auburn Wolfe Publishing, 1983. This is one of these how-to-books that contains clear expositions of tools and techniques for pulling in information about people.

How to Get Anything on Anybody, Book II, Lee Lapin, San Mateo, CA, ISECO, Inc., 1991. This is a revision of the previous edition. Very good to have.

How To Investigate By Computer: 1991, Ralph D. Thomas, Austin, TX, Thomas Publications, 1991. This book is a very clear, nuts-and-bolts explanation of how private investigators can gather information on practically anyone who's ever been listed in a computer. Practically everyone in this country has been.

How To Use Mail Drops For Privacy and Profit, Jack Luger, Port Townsend, WA, Loompanics Unlimited, 1988. A study of how mail drops work, their purposes, and how to make both legal and illegal use of them.

Low Profile, William Petrocelli, NY, McGraw-HIll, 1981. A practical manual on how to reduce the amount of information about yourself available to both official and private investigators.

No Place To Hide, Alan LeMond and Ron Fry, NY, St. Martin's Press, 1975. This is another book showing how private and official investigators are gathering information about everyone they can.

On Target, February 1, 1964. The Minuteman Newsletter. This issue contains a practical description and instructions for opening files on subversives. Although this was written before computers became widespread, the techniques outlined are practical guides to basic information gathering.

Privacy in America, David F. Linowes, Chicago, IL, University of Illinois Press, 1989. This is a description of legal and moral issues of privacy, written from the viewpoint that there is too much privacy invasion by both official and private agencies.

Report of the Warren Commission on the Assassination of President Kennedy, NY, Bantam Books, 1964. This is an extremely valuable sourcebook that contains a variety of information on protective techniques, assassins, techniques of investigation, and intelligence gathering. Unfortunately, many people have never read this book possibly because they disagree with its conclusions. Whether you agree or not about the Kennedy assassination, you can glean a tremendous amount of tangential information from this volume.

The Rise of the Computer State, David Burnham, NY, Random House, 1983. This is an account of how computers are changing the face of information management, and the effect upon privacy.

Security Management, November 1990, Pages 11A-12A. This article details how it's now possible to control a person's access to a building or facility, and the areas to which he's allowed access within. It also shows how it's possible to track a person throughout a suitably equipped facility.

Under Cover: Police Surveillance in America, Gary T. Marx, Berkeley, CA, University of California Press, 1988. This is a civil-rightist account of police surveillance, particularly infiltration of political groups, and the threats of civil liberties.

Understanding U.S. Identity Documents, John Q. Newman, Port Townsend, WA, Loompanics Unlimited, 1991. A practical guide to how official documentation works.

Index

YOU WILL ALSO WANT TO READ:

☐ **55090 BE YOUR OWN DICK: Private Investigating Made Easy,** *by John Q. Newman.* Most detective work involves simple research you can do for yourself — if you know where to look. This book will teach you how to find out everything about your target's finances, health, employment, pastimes and "past lives." If you want to know whether someone is rich or a deadbeat, whether they're on the level or a fraud, whether they're cheating on you, stealing from you, or lying to you, then **Be Your Own Dick!** *1992, 5½ x 8½, 113 pp, soft cover. $12.00.*

☐ **58072 ASK ME NO QUESTIONS, I'LL TELL YOU NO LIES: How to Survive Being Interviewed, Interrogated, Questioned, Quizzed, Sweated, Grilled...,** *by Jack Luger.* How to handle any kind of questioning, including police interrogations, job applications, court testimony, polygraph exams, media interviews, and much more. Learn how to condition yourself against the tricks interrogators use to make you talk. *1991, 5½ x 8½, 177 pp, soft cover. $16.95.*

☐ **61129 UNDERSTANDING U.S. IDENTITY DOCUMENTS,** *by John Q. Newman.* The most detailed examination of identity documents ever published. Covers birth certificates, social security cards, drivers licenses and passports. It shows how each document is generated and used and the agencies issuing them. An essential reference for anyone concerned with their official identity and how it is maintained and manipulated. *1991, 8½ x 11, 207 pp, illustrated, soft cover. $25.00.*

☐ **61092 HOW TO USE MAIL DROPS FOR PRIVACY AND PROFIT,** *by Jack Luger.* Mail drops are the number one most important technique for insuring your privacy. They are confidential mailing addresses that allow you to receive and send mail anonymously. How to select a mail drop; How to run a mail drop; Dodging creditors; Private safe deposit boxes; Sex in the mail; Fake ID; Financial privacy; Electronic mail drops; "Branch" offices; And much more. *1988, 5½ x 8½, 112 pp, illustrated, soft cover. $12.50.*

And much more! We offer the very finest in controversial and unusual books — please turn to our catalog announcement on the next page.

PP92

LOOMPANICS UNLIMITED
PO Box 1197/Port Townsend, WA 98368

Please send me the titles I have checked above. I have enclosed $ _____ (including $4.00 for shipping and handling of 1 to 3 titles, $6.00 for 4 or more).

Name _____

Address _____

City/State/Zip _____

(Washington residents include 7.8% sales tax.)